# JUMPSTART
## Your
## Awesome
## Film
## Production
## Company

### SARA CALDWELL

ALLWORTH PRESS
NEW YORK

12 11 10 09 08   6 5 4 3 2

Published by Allworth Press
An imprint of Allworth Communications, Inc.
10 East 23rd Street, New York, NY 10010

Cover design by Derek Bacchus
Interior design by
Page composition/typography by
Cover photo credit: production scene inset on sunglasses © Jonathan Day

ISBN: 1-58115-400-3

Library of Congress Cataloging-in-Publication Data

Caldwell, Sara C.
    Jumpstart your awesome film production company/Sara Caldwell.
    p. cm.
    Includes index.
    ISBN 1-58115-400-3 (pbk.)
1. Motion pictures–Production and direction.   2. Motion picture industry–Finance.   I. Title.

PN1995.9P.7C26 2005
791.4302'32–dc22

                                                                          2004030123
Printed in the United States of America

# Table of Contents

To all those brave filmmakers
who know you can,
even when they say
you can't.

# Acknowledgments

Thanks to Tad Crawford, publisher, and Nicole Potter, editor, of Allworth Press for their belief and encouragement in the development of this book. I also greatly appreciate Michael Madole's efforts with the promotion.

My immense gratitude for the film production company owners and other experts who generously shared their experience, insights, and wisdom: Joni Brander, Brander Broadcast Consulting; Jamey Brumfield and David Birdwell, Your Plan B; Carole Dean, From the Heart Productions; Ruben Dua, Amaze Films; Shuli Eshel, Eshel Productions; Emma Farrell, Six Foot High Films; Robert Hardy, Rainforest Films; Michael Harpster, Marketing & Distribution Expert; Frey Hoffman, Freydesign Productions; Leslie Kussman, Aquarius Productions; Larry Lundin, CPA; Ruba Nadda, Coldwater Productions; Bill Plympton, Plymptoons; Kerry Rock and Georgina Willis, Potoroo Films; Diana Sole, MotionMasters; Brad Sykes, Nightfall Pictures; Les Szekely, Secret's Out Productions; Chip Taylor, Chip Taylor Communications; and Jerry Vasilatos, Nitestar Productions. Also thanks to Jim Machin of R.duke Productions, an old friend who shared some special memories for this book.

Personal thanks to family and friends for their constant encouragement and support. Very special thanks to my parents, Robert and Pilar Coover, for modeling a world in which anything is possible, and to my children, Dylan and Chloe, for keeping me grounded. Thanks also to independently minded pals Joni Brander, Cathleen Fox, Katherine Bulovic, April Victory, Sunni Boswell, and Jessica Frank for buoying my spirits through the tough spots; also to all my other friends and colleagues, in particular Nelly Leon-Chisen and Denene Harper at the American Hospital Association for their belief in me for so many years. It truly means a lot!

I also want to acknowledge Daniel Bassill, President and CEO of the Cabrini Connections tutor/mentor program in Chicago, who opened my eyes in so many important ways. Thanks to Dan, I have enjoyed one of the most important friendships of my life with my former tutee, the talented and remarkable Isaiah Brooms. As a veteran of mentoring programs and a man who knows no bounds when it comes to selfless giving, Dan is a true role model and hero, no matter what your profession.

> ► 15% of royalties from this book are being donated to Cabrini Connections (*www.tutormentorconnection.org*).

# Introduction

As humans, we are by nature storytellers with a strong yearning to recount our experiences to others in order to make sense of them. Storytellers remind us, through drama or laughter, of what binds us together while teaching important values, traditions, and histories. Gifted storytellers have the power to persuade our thinking and shape our beliefs, and there is no more powerful media in modern society than the visual storytelling of film. It is hardly a surprise that scores of people are drawn to share their stories this way, despite the inherent uncertainty, chances of rejection, and improbable odds for success.

A storyteller at heart, I aspired to have my own production company while working full-time as a producer/writer for various organizations, from a small production company in West Virginia to a mammoth government television agency in Washington, DC. I envisioned myself scripting and producing socially relevant documentaries and inspiring features. I also imagined a world free of nine-to-five obligations, mundane meetings, unbearable commutes, office politics, and micro-management. I knew of others who had ventured out with such a dream, but could it ever really happen for me? For one, I was completely clueless about the business process of starting a company. How could I support myself without a steady paycheck? Who would fund my creative projects? Once made, who would purchase and distribute them? Bottom line, did I have the guts?

As I searched the annals of the library (this was before the wonders of the Internet) I found few resources of value. There were plenty of books on starting a business but none that dealt specifically with the film industry. My research only brought about more questions. Did I need a business plan? Would I be taken seriously without the latest equipment and staffing? Should I look for investors for my projects or would I be committing myself to financial obligations way over my head?

I decided the best course of action was to go straight to the horse's mouth and talk to those who had had already braved what I was contemplating. Fortunately, I had a number of friends who had started their own production companies, and their sage advice was worth more than all the volumes of the library's business section.

I finally took the plunge and formed Amphion Productions, originally founded in Chicago in 1991 and years later moved to Los Angeles. I chose the name because Amphion was a Greek mythological figure credited for building the walls of Thebes by charming the stones into place with his lyre. I had little more than charm with which to start a company—$500 in the bank, an old Apple computer, a fax machine, and one corporate media client. Like Amphion, I was building from nothing but talent and imagination.

I set up shop in my apartment on Chicago's north side, in a tiny room with a window facing a hackberry tree that experts now claim might be the oldest one living in the city. The durable hackberry is able to withstand dry, acid or alkaline soils, windy conditions, and city grime, making it perfect for urban conditions. I wondered if Amphion Productions could be as durable. That tough old tree gave me solace and inspiration as I watched its green leaves change to the autumn hues of orange and red, then winter brown. As the seasons passed outside my window, my knowledge about what it takes to run a production company grew, much of it through trial and error. It's been well over a decade since Amphion Productions' humble beginnings, and I'm happy to say, just like the old hackberry, we're still standing.

Over the years many filmmakers began asking *me* for advice about starting a production company. I found myself repeating the same tips time and again. Thus, the idea for this book was formed. But my words are not enough. As Canadian filmmaker Ruda Nadda of Coldwater Productions in Toronto states, "There are no distinctive rules for starting a film production company, and everyone who has tried has found a different road to success."

"There's not just one method or way to go," says Ruba. "Each filmmaker needs to create his own path and come up with a fresh way of making films and getting them out there."

Like Ruba, every other filmmaker in this book has trod an individual road, wild and untamed or calm and directed. Rob Hardy started Rainforest Films as an engineering student who had never taken a film class, let alone knew what a film camera looked like; likewise, Kerry Rock and Georgina Willis had no formal training before jumpstarting Potoroo Films in Australia to produce innovative shorts and features; Emma Farrell from England dove into Six Foot High Films with a prestigious degree and high ambition but minimal business knowledge; Bill Plympton sold belts on the streets of Manhattan before his Oscar-nominated explosion into the independent animation world; Frey Hoffman began Freydesign Productions in Chicago with little more than a logo and business card; and Jerry Vasilatos used settlement money from a horrific injury case to produce a Lifetime Television Christmas drama through Nitestar Productions in Los Angeles.

This book includes a diverse range of voices from around the world; voices of ordinary individuals with extraordinary dreams who were brave enough to take the risks and face the fears that owning a film production company entail. I believe, like me, you will learn best from those in the trenches if you are serious about starting your own company. As you will read, all of the participants' stories are unique but there are common threads that bind these folks, including a true passion and belief in their craft combined with business know-how and pure gumption.

If you decide to start your own company there will be no guarantee of success and (if you're at all like me) you will make countless mistakes in the process. But what guarantees are there in life, wherever we find ourselves? The point of taking such a risk should not be dependent on your future success but the present reality of living such a dream.

To anyone traveling the vacillating, sometimes bittersweet but wondrous road of filmmaking, I wish you the stars and beyond.

—SARA CALDWELL

# PART I

# FROM DREAM TO REALITY

# CHAPTER 1

# The Pros and Cons of Starting a Film Production Company

*"Making a film is probably the bravest thing you'll ever do in your life."*

KERRY ROCK, POTOROO FILMS, SYDNEY, AUSTRALIA

W hat storyteller hasn't imagined seeing her creative vision on the big screen? The appeal of movie-making as a visual narrative form has been the ambition of millions, as an increasing number of film festivals around the world attest. Filmmakers are compelled, heart and soul, to share their unique stories in a way that parallels human experience, whether through drama, comedy, action, horror, romance, real life, or experimentation.

With such heartfelt drive, many choose the difficult and uncertain path of a filmmaking career by operating under a company banner, sacrificing significant financial and emotional stability in pursuit of the dream.

Most creative types, such as filmmakers, are right-brain oriented–random, intuitive, subjective–versus the logical, rational, and analytical left-brain type. My own mental abilities lean heavily to the right, which I've learned can be a wonderful asset and a serious detriment. When venturing into company ownership, right-brainers often neglect the inherent business aspects, which can easily consume over 50 percent of our working hours.

"The enormity of the information I had to learn was a huge challenge," reflects Emma Farrell of Six Foot High Films in Brighton, England. "After spending my life in education I was suddenly in the business world and had to learn about health and safety, accounts, VAT, and the Inland Revenue; very technical administrative things. But looking back on the fears I faced, I think I was able to do it because I didn't really know about the enormities I was undertaking. It's the entrepreneurial spirit of going blindly forward and saying *yay*, I'm going to start my own production company and make films! If I had actually known what it was going to involve I might have been more circumspect."

As Emma expressed, the business side of owning a company can be daunting. It helps to ask yourself some basic questions about why and how you are going to start your company. It is a process of self-evaluation as well as pondering concrete realities.

## Why I Started My Company

There are many reasons for starting a production company. Some aspire to make features or documentaries, while others want to build a company that offers a wide array of production services.

If you take a look at the people who *are* the material of this book you'll see a variety of incentives and ambitions. Jerry Vasilatos of Nitestar Productions in Los Angeles is mainly focused on editing projects with his Avid system to make a living and support his independent projects. Diana Sole of MotionMasters in Charleston, West Virginia, established her company to provide services to commercial, corporate, and nonprofit clients in the region. Bill Plympton in New York City formed Plymptoons as a business entity through which to produce and distribute his independent animations. Les Szekely started Secrets Out Productions in Los Angeles as a writer, hoping a company banner would give his partner and himself more prestige.

"We all know that if you call a studio and said hey, I'm a writer, I want to come pitch some ideas to you, they're basically going to tell you no," says Les. "But if you say I'm so-and-so from so-and-so productions. Can we come in and pitch some projects to you, most of the time they'll let you come in and at least pitch some with their development exec.

So that's why I started Secret's Out Productions. Once digital video came out, I started making films with the same company name."

The reason for starting a company can be personally, financially, geographically, and/or esoterically motivated. It doesn't hurt to ask yourself, why do I want to start a film production company? The answer will be a starting focal point.

## Pros and Cons

A good place to begin when considering starting a company is to look at the advantages and disadvantages. There are many pros and cons, a few of which are listed below. If you find that the cons seem insurmountable, you may want to reevaluate the timing of your decision. However, there is never a perfect world in which to take such a risk, and you could end up waiting for a moment that never happens. Listen to your intuition as you read this list.

Frey Hoffman, owner of Freydesign Productions in Chicago, sums up a common perspective on the pros and cons.

"The fact that no one is really dictating your work is exciting, plus you're able to pursue work you find meaningful. Being your own boss is a very big deal. The huge disadvantage is not having a steady paycheck, but you learn to adapt to it over time. Hours can also be extremely grueling because once you get work or start your own project you can find yourself going around the clock. There's always something else you can do for your business. The challenge is figuring out an appropriate rhythm, knowing when to stop, and learning to say, 'I'll do more tomorrow.' "

Many filmmakers worry that location is an issue. If you don't live in a major city, does a film production company even have a chance? Les Szeleky of Secret's Out Productions recently moved from Los Angeles to Cleveland and couldn't care less about the geographical change.

"If you want to make independent films on shoestring budgets you can be anywhere," says Les. "It's not like 90 percent of us are in L.A. and the other 10 percent someplace else. It's really the other way around. Hollywood is not so much about filmmaking but about making money. Granted there's nothing wrong with wanting to make money but

| PROS | CONS |
|---|---|
| Being your own boss | You must make all the decisions and wear multiple hats |
| Income is potentially unlimited | No steady paycheck, health insurance, or retirement plan |
| Time to work on your own film projects | You are responsible and accountable for the success or failure of a project |
| Freedom to make your own schedule | You must be disciplined enough to work autonomously |
| New opportunities arise through meeting and networking with other professionals | Marketing and business skills are as necessary as creative abilities |
| You decide on team members for a film project | You may feel isolated and cut off from the normal world |
| Executive creative control on most projects | You have no technical support or assistants unless you pay for them |
| Ability to create a name for yourself in the film industry | Potential for failure and embarrassment |
| Interesting work and lifestyle | Competition is fierce |
| Prestige and funding opportunities with successful projects | Funding for film projects is extremely difficult to acquire |

very often the big multi-blockbuster world of Hollywood overshadows any attempt to be creative or different. Every now and then you see a movie that's genuinely good but more often it's a letdown. Only time will tell where it's going to go but independent filmmakers are certainly all over the place and don't have to answer to anybody but ourselves. If our films make it, that's great. If they don't, well, we did it our way and the mistakes were ours."

The biggest fear of any independent filmmaker is how to survive without a steady paycheck. Encountering slow times is an overwhelming challenge that has caused many filmmakers to give up on their dreams.

"You're not going to make a living overnight making movies," Les Szekely points out. "If so, it's going to be a very long Alaskan night."

When Jim Machin started R.duke Productions in 1988 as a director and videographer, he spent sixth months on an extensive marketing campaign that included eight-hour days of making phone calls to prospective clients and sending out hundreds of letters and postcards. One morning, he looked at his contact list and realized he had made every initial and follow-up call he could without having landed a single job.

"I remember very distinctly making that last call. It was noon and there was nothing else I could do. It was my first realization that when there's nothing to do, you should just go have fun. Go to the beach, go swimming, whatever. The first job I finally got was through a friend. All I did was pick up a tape, take it to a dub house and get four copies. The total bill was $60 but I was so thrilled because I made $20 and I figured it was a start. Strangely, the next day the phone rang and I got a bigger job. And suddenly the jobs started pouring in."

Jim's optimism kept him going at a point where others might have succumbed, and I'm happy to report, more than fifteen years later, that R.duke Productions is still thriving.

Struggling through the slow times can be demoralizing, and it's not exclusive to startups. Companies with many years in business discover such debilitating moments. Diana Sole, president of MotionMasters of Charleston, West Virginia, and the producer of numerous documentary and corporate projects, recalls one especially frightful time.

"We have slow cycles like anyone. Along about Thanksgiving I'm starting to go crazy because business drops off so significantly, but after fifteen years I realize that's going to happen. I try to prepare myself for it but each year these knots begin to form in my stomach. The worst was after 9/11. For a small company in West Virginia you'd wonder how the terrorists could affect us, but we lost about half of the business we had on the books. We'd come together as a staff on Monday mornings and I'd look around the table and see ten other people sitting there, knowing about each of their families very closely, and I would worry about how to keep all those paychecks going. We ended up weathering that storm pretty well."

Despite the slow times, there are certainly enough positives to sustain us. Autonomy and freedom of schedule probably top the list.

When I started Amphion Productions in 1991, after eight years as a company workhorse, I was thrilled not to have to get up at the crack of dawn, commute in unbearable traffic, play office politics, and attend butt-numbing meetings. I could work in my cutoffs, bang away on scripts, or chat on the phone to friends without worrying about who was looking over my shoulder. Ultimately, I could create my own destiny.

Every filmmaker in this book has been around for more than a few years, and it's the exhilaration that comes from the high points along with grit and determination that has kept their companies afloat and flourishing.

## Types of Film Production Companies

Film production companies can be structured in a number of ways, mostly determined by financial circumstances. Many startups can't subside on their "in-house" creative projects alone, at least in the beginning, and depend on offering script, production, and post-production services to commercial and corporate clients.

Information on various business structures are described in chapter 3. Following is a synopsis of the most typical film production company types:

### One Man Band

This is how many filmmakers begin, typically working out of their home with limited resources. When Frey Hoffman of Freydesign Productions in Chicago created his company in 1997, he had little more than a business card and computer.

"I didn't even formally legalize it.," says Frey. "Basically I came up with a logo and put it on a business card and that was about the extent of it. And a strong desire to work in film and video."

There is no need to legalize a company if it is a sole proprietorship bearing your name (e.g., John Doe & Associates or Jane Smith Productions), but if you use a fictitious name you must go through a simple registration and announcement process that is offered by most local newspapers.

## Partnership

In this situation, two or more creative minds come together to form a company. An agreement should be signed between the partners to avoid assumptions about roles and responsibilities.

In 1995, longtime friends Kerry Rock and Georgina Willis formed Potoroo Films in Sydney, Australia, with the goal of making experimental short and feature length films.

"We initially had a partnership agreement drawn up," says Kerry. "The first partnership agreement was about who was responsible for each task. We also made sure we had all the business side of the company lined up, like copyright issues, as we realized we needed structures in place for taxes and other such things. As soon as you start making films, even shorts, you have to be more business oriented and have all those pieces in place."

## Project-Specific Company

Sometimes filmmakers form a short-term company, such as a limited partnership, with the goal of completing a specific independent film project, which is necessary when working with investors. When screenwriter/director Jerry Vasilatos set out to shoot his first feature *Solstice* in Chicago, he formed Nitestar Productions to have a company through which to operate during production.

"When I started making the movie I wasn't formally a corporation," explains Jerry. "I was just a guy making a movie and had to be under the banner of a production company, as it really helped in terms of working with vendors and distributors."

After *Solstice* was complete, Jerry decided to formalize his company as a corporation. He has since directed, edited, and produced multiple projects through Nitestar Productions, Inc.

## Full-Service Company

With finances out of the gate or built over time, some film production companies are able to offer a full array of services, from scripting and production to post. As such, they typically form a type of corporation. These companies usually make their profits on client services to help offset the overhead of equipment and staffing.

MotionMasters of West Virginia depends predominantly on corporate clients while producing a unique slate of documentaries on the side.

"I've always enjoyed working on the corporate side of video productions because you get to learn a little bit about so many different types of businesses or industries," says MotionMasters' president Diana Sole. "So from an interest level I think corporate work can be very stimulating. It also gives you the ability to practice your craft and make a living while you're doing it."

## Staying Focused

One piece of advice that many filmmakers shared: Understand that it is going to be a very long process to get your company and independent film projects off the ground.

Brad Sykes, a Los Angeles director of numerous horror and thriller features, recalls his naïvety when he started out.

"I did a twenty-minute short in the no-budget Robert Rodriguez style of filmmaking. My friend and I were convinced that since I had the short and had some scripts, we were definitely going to get the financing for a feature. There was no way that that wasn't going to happen. And it didn't happen."

As Brad painfully learned, starting a company with the intention of getting rich quick off film or script sales will lead to disappointment when results don't come fast enough.

"If your desire is to make a quick buck, go play the stock market," suggests Rob Hardy of Rainforest Films in Atlanta, Georgia. "Filmmaking is a labor of love and that's what sustains you during difficult periods. You have to be a risk-taker because no one's going to take a risk on you but *you*. You can complain all you want about opportunities passing you by, but the only way they will really happen is if you create them for yourself."

In 1996 Jerry Vasilatos moved Nitestar Productions from Chicago to Los Angeles in search of better opportunities. He has learned that success takes patience and tenacity, especially in the city of dreams.

"I see so many people do this because they want to get rich and become celebrities. That's not a good reason. You should do this because you love it and the financial rewards in the long term will hopefully show up. Jumping into filmmaking with the intention of becoming famous is so narcissistic and rarely happens overnight. You can't come out to Hollywood and say I'm going to give myself a year and if it doesn't work I'm leaving. I've been out here since '96 and am constantly asked by my Mom, 'How long before you decide you've given it enough time and you're going to look for something else?' I say never, because I wouldn't be happy doing anything else and I've already invested too much time to give myself a deadline to say if it doesn't happen by the end of this year, I have to find something else. Many people who have become successful may have been trying for ten or fifteen years. But they kept their goal in mind. You've got to be in it for the long haul and see it through."

As Jerry acknowledged, it is not unusual to get discouragement from others, whether through honest concern or jealousy. Unfortunately, one negative remark can cut deeper than a hundred praises. When the road is full of such potholes, it helps to remember why you are pursuing your dream in the first place.

"Most people around you have not gone through the process of starting a company and never will," says Joni Brander of Brander Broadcast Consulting. "When I'd tell my Mom about a new client, she would say, 'Maybe they'll offer you a real job.' It was funny but very upsetting to me at the time. After twelve years she's learned not to say that, because we didn't speak for a week the first time, but she still doesn't get it. I think there's also a certain amount of jealousy from some people, wanting you to feel bad or lazy. One of the shifts you have to make is that sometimes you'll be working a ton and sometimes you don't have to. And that's a good thing. That's why you do it. So it's important not to let other people put their stuff on you about how you should be living your life."

Emma Farrell of Six Foot High Films advises, "If you really, really love this, you can make it happen. The number of disasters I've survived is just farcical, so just be fully prepared for things to go hysterically and spectacularly wrong."

## Finding Support

Even if you are forming a company by yourself, you don't have to manage everything alone. It is important to seek help, especially in areas you might be uncomfortable with.

"When I first started MotionMasters I had a conversation with the man who was going to be our accountant," recalls Diana Sole. "I said, 'I don't know anything about which column to put the money on the books, but what I do know is how to produce great work and take care of my clients and I can do that and make money at it. Now you tell me where to put the money on the books.' He laughed and said, 'Diana, this is going to work very well!' You have to find people of integrity who will be as committed to excellence in their craft as you are and just move forward. I shudder when I look back at all the things I didn't know that I should have known. I just fumbled along and made a lot of mistakes. But I did what I could with the knowledge I had and learned when to seek the advice of others."

Emma Farrell concurs.

"Take as many business courses as you can but do not be afraid to ask for advice even if you think you sound like a complete idiot."

Chicago CPA Larry Lundin offers practical advice for connecting with the right experts.

"I feel that anyone getting into business should have at least three professionals: an attorney, accountant, and insurance agent. You want these professionals to be comfortable enough to talk to one another and make sure that they're all advising you in the right direction."

Starting your own production company involves introspection on the pros and cons, seeking professional advice, and knowing that you have the passion to carry things through for the long term. There will be many fears, trials, and mistakes. But after reading about the film-makers in this book, you will see that with belief, talent, and tenacity any dream is attainable.

# CHAPTER 2

# Extreme Ambition

*"Don't dwell on rejection as negative feedback. It's their loss, just move on."*

EMMA FARRELL, SIX FOOT HIGH FILMS, BRIGHTON, ENGLAND

I have always found that the most intriguing filmmakers are those who have unusual passions and interests beyond celluloid. When I interviewed Emma Farrell of Six Foot High Films, our conversation revolved around her company history, film projects, and advice to other filmmakers. Only later did I discover that she is a freediver who placed third in the British championships. It explained a lot about her tenacity; surely anyone who can hold her breath for four minutes and twenty-one seconds at frighteningly dangerous oceanic depths wouldn't blink an eye at the challenges of movie-making.

"Filmmaking and freediving are both fairly unusual and involve risk and a high level of control," says Emma. "You can't make a mistake when you freedive so you have to be totally focused. Filmmaking is similar in that I strive for perfection and that means concentrating on making sure hundreds of variables come together in the right way, though if I mess up there isn't usually the risk of death!"

Emma has always been drawn to filmmaking as an appealing medium through which to express her unique talents and imagination.

Emma Farrell (center) on location with *Homecoming*. (© Jonathan Day.)

"When I grew up I did a lot of acting, writing, painting, and music, and in film you've got words, dialogue, emotion, and pictures and it's a way to converge all my artistic talents into telling stories. As a writer and director, I love creating so much through a little dialogue and telling a story with juxtaposing images. What I've written can be made visually deeper and more complex. In my films everything you see out of the corner of your eye is chosen for a reason, and I love watching other people's films and searching for that kind of close attention to things that are part of the character and story."

## Six Foot High Films

Freshly armed with a Master's Degree in documentary filmmaking, Emma formed Six Foot High Films (a reflection of her height) in 1998 and began production on her first feature film, *Into the Light*.

"I was actually inspired by a book called the *Guerrilla Film-maker's Handbook* for people who decide they're going to make their feature on no budget whatsoever," recalls Emma. "So I started down that road with a script and had to form a company to get it made. In the beginning there was no company structure. In England you have to have a director and a secretary to start a company, so I was the director and a friend of a friend was the company secretary. Unfortunately, she didn't realize quite what hard work filmmaking is and after we'd shot the first part of the feature, she left. So then there was just me. As far as a business plan, I had gone to a business course and had constructed a plan, but it was very connected to the film we were shooting. Now the company mission is focused on long-term growth, with feature films being our goal."

Emma's features and shorts are an evocative blend of unsettling foreboding and comedy. Her twelve-minute 35-mm film *Cupboard Love* is a dark tale of female friendship, chocolate spread, and sharp knives. Cut close to the bone, it is guaranteed to keep you perched on the edge of your seat until the final twist in the tale. *Cupboard Love* received the Gold Special Jury Award at WorldFest-Houston in 2003.

Emma's ninety-second 35-mm film *A Small Death* depicts a young girl lying feverish in a candlelit room, reliving a devastating encounter in an idyllic garden. The story plays on biblical and folklore themes to present a journey from light into darkness through the loss of innocence.

"All of our shorts are done for the express purpose of showing the world how good we are," says Emma. "However, in addition to satisfying my creativity, they've been tremendous learning experiences. I get bored very, very easily and if I had to wait years to get a feature off the ground without doing anything else, I'd go insane. If I haven't worked on anything for a while, I'll just write another short, or shoot a silly film with friends. I have to keep working."

Emma's short films primarily get shown at film festivals and at industry screenings in London. "It's *very* difficult to make money from short films," Emma acknowledges, "but not impossible. The most I have known anyone to make was 7,000 UK pounds due to the fact they sold all rights to HBO. However, the contract was negotiated by a short film distributor, and the filmmaker in question has yet to see any of the money. Although I haven't made a penny from the short films, the exposure generated has been worth its weight in gold!"

## Commercial Work

Because it has not been possible to make a living from making short films, Emma has leaned on commercial and corporate work to financially support her creative efforts.

"The past year about 90 percent of the work has been commercial and corporate work, which has funded the ongoing administration of the company and entering film festivals, shipping films to festivals, and for developing our features. So everything is funded by the commercial and corporate work."

Emma's commercials can be as haunting as her personal slate of films. She directed a ninety-second spot called *Lost* for the Propaganda agency. Paying reference to *Don't Look Now* and *Schindler's List*, a man in a shopping center announces that he has "lost his little girl" and we follow his drama to a shocking conclusion. Propaganda's creative editor had an enthusiastic response after seeing the rough cut—"F***ing brilliant! F***ing brilliant! I've shown it to three people and they've all burst into tears!"

The commercial was announced winner of "Best Low Budget TV" at the Cream Awards in 2002 and the National Adline Grand Prix in 2003.

Grit and determination have been the cornerstone of Emma's success, helping her hold her breath when funding wasn't coming through the door.

"The more you go through difficult times, the easier it is. You just have to be realistic and think okay, I didn't get the funding, it doesn't matter. I'll find another way to do this. I could have given up so many times and it's entirely because of sheer force of energy and determination that the company would not go down."

## Multiple Projects

Part of Emma's strategy is to have multiple projects in development, so her eggs aren't all in one basket.

"You need to have so many things going at once," she suggests. "You've got to do the effort with some assuredness that most things won't work. You have to work really hard and never, ever give up. When I first started, the whole crew consisted of *me*. I believe in order to succeed you need an unshakeable belief in your ideas. It doesn't matter if you shoot a project with your Mum's video camera. If it's good, it will prevail. You also have to be open to the ideas of others. If you're open, your own ideas will be magnified tenfold. Linking to that, you need to remember that film is a subjective medium. If one person thinks your film is rubbish, there will be ten who think it's wonderful, and often they'll be complete strangers."

While started in Manchester, Six Foot High Films relocated to Brighton, considered England's premiere holiday destination for a seaside escape. Emma likens the experience of a filmmaker to turning stones on Brighton's pebbled beaches.

"You turn over every single pebble in the hope that one will hold a diamond because you'll get rejections with every project. Disappointments without exception will outweigh all the successes you have. You must totally forget them if they're bad."

## Homecoming

After self-funding all of her own projects, Emma was thrilled to finally discover a diamond in the form of 30,000 pounds to produce her fifteen-minute 35-mm Cinemascope film *Homecoming*, a heartrending tale of family, love, and loss. In the story, a young girl, Tadine, is a long way from home and wants to return to Kosova and her beloved dog, Kostandin. Adrift in a new country, her mother tries to hold the family together as the father sinks deeper into his own despair, unable to help his only child. Tadine's determination to get the family home and the friendship of a boy next door finally forces her father to confront his demons, heal his past, and help his daughter find peace and a future in their new home.

"The money for *Homecoming* came from a big production company called Piper Films," explains Emma. "They believed in the script enough to fund the entire project, which was just fantastic, especially as the script had been turned down twice for public funding. If Piper Films hadn't come in, this film would never have been made."

Production still from *Homecoming*.

Emma doesn't believe she got the funding by chance, but due to extensive effort invested in networking and building relationships.

"I would say networking is the most important thing and the thing I hate most, because I feel uncomfortable and it's not really in my personality," she admits. "However, just to show how much it works, *Homecoming* was made purely due to relationship building. I told a producer who was working on product placement that I'd started my company and we talked about a feature I wanted to do at the time. We spoke about four times on the phone and then ran into each other a few years ago in Cannes after some guy spilled his drink down the pair of us, and we realized we knew each other. We developed a friendship from that. Tiffany, the producer, was blown away by my script and she made it happen."

While filmmaking is a challenge, there's no doubt that someone who has tackled the perilous and extreme sport of freediving would exhilarate in the thrill of such a complex and uncertain career. I expect we'll continue to see amazing things from Emma Farrell, under water and on-screen.

# CHAPTER 3

# The Business of Starting a Company

*"You can't lose track of quality of life issues. Did you decide to start your own company to work 24/7 or because you wanted a better life?"*

LARRY LUNDIN, CPA, CHICAGO

Since starting my own production company, I have come to appreciate a totally different brand of hero than we're accustomed to on the silver screen. While fictional heroes might save the universe from impending cataclysms, there is an underappreciated and often comically maligned underdog who deserves our trust and gratitude. Although never portrayed as a gun-toting barbarian, this brand of hero has guided me through some tense white-knuckle moments come tax season and the financial guillotine of April 15.

Good accountants can be heroes to any new company owner, saving hundreds or even thousands of dollars in ways that filmmakers might easily overlook if trying to manage their own finances. When I started Amphion Productions in Chicago, I naively picked an accountant from the Yellow Pages, which was an utter disaster. He didn't understand my business, sold me on services I didn't need, and I lost more than a few shirts through general neglect at tax time.

I was *his* client, but he wasn't invested in *me* or my company's best interests.

A few excruciatingly expensive lessons later, a friend referred me to Lawrence (Larry) Lundin, a CPA with an impeccable history of serving clients with integrity and personalized attention.

Although it is hard to imagine Larry in a mask and cape, he has always been there at my beck and call to advise and help me improve my business. Cape or not, he is grounded, knowledgeable, and invested in my company's success, as any good accountant should be.

Larry Lundin, CPA.

Larry's first rule of thumb is that you treat your business *as* a business rather than a hobby.

"A lot of people don't realize that if they're going to be in business they should treat it as a business and keep everything separate from their personal accounts. Co-mingling funds is not illegal but it's stupid. What type of entity the business should be is something to discuss with your attorney and accountant; whether you're a sole proprietorship or partner with somebody, incorporated, or become an LLC. There are options as far as the entity, but you still want to start with a business mindset and keep things separate."

The entities that Larry mentioned include three main options: sole proprietorship, partnership, and corporation. There is plenty of information about these structures on the Internet and at the library, and an attorney or legal advisor can guide you in the best direction for your particular needs.

In brief, a **sole proprietorship** is the easiest and least expensive way to start a company. You can operate a sole proprietorship from a home or office with minimal fees for the business name registration and fictitious name certificate. Your local newspaper can manage these logistics for you for a nominal fee.

| ADVANTAGES | DISADVANTAGES |
|---|---|
| Easy and inexpensive to get started | Company growth is limited to personal ambition and resources |
| Control over your own decisions | You have to make all decisions alone |
| Tax ease and advantages | Family or personal affairs and assets can get easily mixed with the business |

**Partnerships** come in various forms, the most common being general partnerships and limited partnerships. A *general partnership* is when two or more people form a company with an oral or written agreement, although it is advisable to draw up a partnership agreement that establishes roles, responsibilities, spending, and profit-sharing. Each partner is liable for *all* the firm's debts, as well as each other's actions.

*Limited partnerships* are most commonly used by filmmakers who need a short-term company for a specific project. A limited partnership is one in which some of the partners (e.g., investors) have a limited liability to the company's creditors. For filmmakers, this provides a way to raise money from investors without involving them in the day-to-day operations and does not require the forming of a corporation or issuing stock. For example, Jane Doe plans to produce a $1 million independent feature. She lacks the cash to produce the film herself so she creates a limited partnership to seek others who are willing to invest for an interest in returns. Jane sells twenty limited partnership interests for $50,000 each to cover the cost of the project.

However, investors need to question whether the high economic risk of investing in such a company can be sustained. While investors are not liable for any business debts, the company partners are also not liable for paying back any investments if the business fails.

A **corporation** is the most complex structure and you don't want to travel this road without good legal counsel at your side. The type of corporation you select may depend on the size of your business, the number of partners or shareholders, and business assets. My company is a small, closely held "S" corporation, versus a "C" or regular

| ADVANTAGES | DISADVANTAGES |
| --- | --- |
| Shared responsibilities resulting in time savings | Disputes over decisions and sharing of tasks |
| Combined skills and resources | Responsibility for other partner's business actions |
| Tax ease and advantages | No clear line of authority in general partnership compared to individually owned company |

corporation. An "S" corporation offers limited liability for the corporate shareholder, but you pay income taxes on the same basis as a sole proprietor or partnership. In comparison, "C" corporation is taxed on business profits, and the owners pay individual income tax only on money they draw from the corporation as a salary, bonus, or dividend. Many entrepreneurs are now opting for limited liability companies (LLC). As with "S" corporations, incomes from these companies are passed through the owners and reported on the owners' personal income tax returns, thus eliminating the double taxation of a company and individual.

Unlike "S" corporations, LLCs offer more flexibility and ease of operation, as there are no restrictions on ownership, and they are not subject to the same formalities as other corporations. For example, LLC owners can distribute profits in any manner they see fit versus regulated profit sharing. Again, your accountant and legal advisor can help you determine the best option and understand the annual requirements.

| ADVANTAGES | DISADVANTAGES |
| --- | --- |
| Separation of personal and business assets | More expensive and complicated to establish |
| Easier to raise capital | Less freedom of activity due to IRS regulations |
| Foundation for growing larger | Legal and tax formalities |

## Well-Laid Plans

"I definitely think planning is an issue and the scary thing you hear when you start a business is that you should do a business plan," says Larry. "You'll look at these business plans out there that are an inch thick and done by an MBA and you're going, 'I can't do that and I won't even think about it.' I always tell people a business plan can start out small and simple. It can just be a notebook where you start putting your ideas before you start your business. It might include your mission and what you plan to do, but a business plan should also get into projections. Here's where I think our sales or revenue is going to come from. Here's where I project our revenue to be the first month, three months, six months from now. So planning is key.

"At the same time, so are budgets. If you're leaving a secure job, you need to know your household budget because if you're married or have children, you can't necessarily reduce your income and make your mortgage payment. Take a look at your household budget and what you need to bring in each month to survive. Then you know the minimums. When it comes to the business, what's the gross profit you're going to realize? What costs can or can't you control? If you have to get an office, what's your rent going to be? Can you operate out of an office in the home? Do you need extra equipment or will your existing equipment do for now? If you're going to grow, you also need to set aside some money for acquisitions, whether that's a computer, software, or film equipment.

"So the business plan is something that should be started when you first begin thinking about the business. If you go for financing because you need operating capital or you need capital to buy equipment, the banker will want to know something about you. Unless you have a tremendous home with great equity, the banker's going to want to see your personal financial statement with your assets, liabilities, and net worth. If you walk in with a business plan, whether it's a quarter-inch thick or an inch thick, it should say, 'Here's my experience, my personal history, and why you should lend me money. Here's where I see my business today, here's where I see it in six months. Here's why you *want* to lend me money because you're going to get me to this point.' Bankers are in the business of lending money. If they don't lend money, they don't make money. At the same time, they need to have a reason to lend it to you, and a business plan is a key thing to have as an ongoing tool and, like your business, it constantly changes."

## Creating a Business Plan

A business plan is different than a specific film proposal targeted to investors, although it can be used in such cases to demonstrate the solidity and goals of your company. Following are items that are useful to include in a business plan:

▶ Mission statement (what is the purpose of your company)
▶ Company structure and operations (who is running the show and how)
▶ Company goals and objectives (how many projects you intend to complete, how much revenue you expect to gain, etc.)
▶ Description of planned films or other projects
▶ Budgets and schedules for proposed films/projects
▶ Projection of potential income and funding sources
▶ Marketing and distribution strategies for proposed films/projects

So how do you put all of this information together? Many people start with a mission statement, which defines the vision of the company.

Mission statements are intended to provide a sense of purpose and long-term direction in daily activity. Typically, a mission statement defines a company by describing what it does. Disney's simple mission statement, for example, is "to make people happy." Frey Hoffman of Freydesign Productions has a clear mission.

"My mission is to work with not-for-profit public interest groups. It's not exclusive but for me those groups represent an enduring value to the community at large, which is what I want to contribute toward."

Filmmakers often become so intent on the minutiae of a particular project that they neglect to look at the big picture of where they are headed as a company. Sometimes they don't think they need business tools as they are in a creative field where such things shouldn't apply. But whether you are making steel beams or independent shorts, a focused company mission will help you stay focused on your goals.

Here is another example of a mission statement. The Australian International Documentary Conference (AIDC) provides a market place for documentaries for national and international buyers and distributors, showcases the work of Australian and international documentary makers, and creates a forum to discuss content, craft, technology, and future directions. Their mission statement reads:

"To stage a recurrent international documentary event that is both an inspirational conference and successful marketplace, promoting and furthering the interests of Australian documentary and its makers."

Once you have created a mission statement, the next step is to develop specific goals that support your mission. For example, two of AIDC's goals are to:

- ▶ foster professional development for documentary content creators by providing access to critical debate, analysis, and an energetic forum for the discussion of important issues facing the documentary community;
- ▶ foster industry development by providing a networking and deal-making forum to develop markets for documentary in conventional and emerging technologies.

As you can see in the above example, the mission statement describes the overall purpose of the organization, while the goals are much more specific about the actual functions. As a film production company owner, your mission statement will probably entail a description of the type of film projects you want to produce or clients you hope to solicit. A mission statement should not be created for marketing purposes but to reflect your personal vision of the company. If you create a mission statement that seems generic, it might be an indicator that you have not spent enough time thinking about what makes your company unique.

Following are some questions that will help you define your mission statement:

- ▶ Why are you creating a film production company?
- ▶ Who is your audience or client base?
- ▶ What image do you want your company to convey?
- ▶ What media services (if appropriate) do you provide?
- ▶ How does your company differ from others already in existence?
- ▶ How is modern technology (if appropriate) going to help support your client base?
- ▶ What philosophies or values does your company uphold?

Again, your company goals should specifically describe the actual products or services you plan to provide. For example, to:

- ▶ produce three 30-minute documentaries a year on topics that enhance people's understanding of serious environmental concerns, or
- ▶ provide high-quality, low-cost post-production services to non-profit organizations and educational clients.

One of the toughest challenges of putting together a business plan is the budgeting aspect. How can you possibly predict your potential revenue when just starting out? If your company is client oriented, it is obviously easier as you can use your rate card, calculate the approximate (and realistic) jobs you hope to secure, and draw numbers from that. While it is easy to estimate expenses, it is much harder to anticipate earnings for "creative" projects, especially as it can take years to reap any revenue, if ever. Anticipated revenue sources for these budgets have to include investors, sponsors, grants, and "outside" income from other sources of business, like commercial work. Chances are (and I know from experience) that you won't be completely on the mark with your budget in the first year or two, but as your business grows you will begin to understand realistic expectations and be able to budget accordingly. Regardless, the budget you create will give you concrete financial goals to aim for, as well as an understanding of what is going to disappear from your account.

There are a number of good books on developing business plans and film proposals, such as *Filmmaking & Finance: Business Plans for Independents*, by Louise Levison. However you form your business plan, it is important to review and update it as your company grows and changes. Focused and realistic goals will help keep you from getting sidetracked. Some filmmakers even post their company goals by their desks so as not to lose sight of the "big picture."

## Use Your Time Wisely

Larry concurs that remaining focused and planning the best use of your time is critical.

"You have to sit back and ask yourself, 'Where do I spend my energy? How much time do I have available for the things I want to accomplish?' Time is the one thing you're selling and there's a limit to how much you have. You want to make sure you're allocating it well. And remember, you always have to hold something back for the future. While working on one project, you still have to devote time to networking and getting the next project or opportunity in motion."

When you are ready to set up shop, an accountant and legal advisor can help you determine the best structure. Although you might be excited to get moving with your film projects, take time up front to write a business plan, no matter how simple it starts out, so that you have specific goals and strategies for achieving them. Well-laid plans will keep you headed in the right direction. So says my superhero.

# CHAPTER 4

# The Importance of Planning

*"Everyone I know has worked for nothing for a great period of time. Eventually you realize your skills have come to a point where you can actually get paid."*

FREY HOFFMAN, FREYDESIGN PRODUCTIONS, CHICAGO

I agreed to meet Frey Hoffman on a trip to Chicago after he had sent me a sample reel, as I needed a local shooter for a project. Unfortunately, the night before I had tripped over a garden hose at a friend's house and landed face down on concrete. By the time Frey and I gathered at

Frey Hoffman, founder of Freydesign Productions.
(© Frey Hoffman 2004.)

a small diner in Lincoln Park, my face looked as if it had been used as a punching bag. Frey did his best to ignore my pitiful bruises, and I found him to be intelligent, sensitive, and engaging. I hired him for the project and for many others since then.

Frey's interests have taken him into the technical side of the industry, primarily in camera work and editing. His company, Freydesign Productions, is a Chicago-based, full-service production company, which has produced Frey's own work as well as many projects for diverse clients. But these credits took time to build. When Frey created Freydesign Productions in 1997, he was truly starting from scratch. He had limited working experience and only a few film production courses under his belt. He formed the company while he was still in college, which presented challenges as he did not have much hands-on experience at the onset.

"I had a minimum of skills when I started the production company," says Frey. "But it was enough for me to begin going around and doing some interesting work. There was definitely the fear that if I started to work in film then I obviously couldn't work at a more secure straight job. Would it be enough to sustain me? I started the company, but then I went to Columbia College to get a better base of knowledge in film production. So for a year and a half straight I did every semester I could at Columbia and got a degree there.

"I started to get some small jobs shooting for local sporting events, local parties, and things like that. Once I got my degree I had a much better range of experience. Working with larger lighting packages, video editing, and just a greater base of production knowledge, I started to work as a freelance cameraman."

Up to this point, Frey had made a minimum investment in his business and operated more as a freelancer than company owner. It soon became apparent that he would need to invest more if Freydesign Productions was to be taken seriously. This required some thoughtful planning, as he was working with limited resources.

"I worked without any equipment of my own, just a body of knowledge and contacts, but I started to realize that if I wanted to be taken more seriously I needed to own some equipment. I started off with a camera and then there was one project about a sculptor based out of New York that helped me make the investment to get editing equipment, so I went for it.

Some of that initial investment also came from a partner of mine on a kids' television pilot. We'd cut a trailer for it and we realized, Wow, if we actually paid that costly hourly rate to do the whole episode it would be cheaper to buy our own equipment and have it for other projects. So those were the first two major investments, the camera and editing system."

## How Much Should I Invest in My Company?

There is no right or wrong answer to the question raised above. Much of it will depend on your personal finances. However, a great many production companies have gone by the wayside because of heavy overhead. When I was living in Chicago, a friend was the co-partner of a large production company with an overhead of around $11,000 a month to cover the cost of office space, staffing, equipment, and marketing. At the time, business was good and the company thrived for about five years. But when the recession of 1991 emerged, clients began to disappear. With such a large overhead, the company was just above water in the good times. One year later, my friend was operating as a freelancer in a small apartment while paying off a great deal of debt.

Part of Freydesign's steady growth comes from careful planning and caution about investments, especially in the ever-changing technical world of film and video production.

"If you pick up an industry magazine, about a quarter to a third of it is filled with advertisements for new, cutting-edge equipment," notices Frey. "Especially now there's always some sort of technological improvement from what existed three months before, whether it's on the camera or editing side of things, and I think having a firm grasp of what tools you need to accomplish your job—nothing more and nothing less—is important. So I try not to get sucked into the frenzy of the industry."

There are alternative ways to "look big" while staying small within your financial abilities. Bartering services with other companies or film professionals is a common and effective way to get projects in motion.

"Other filmmakers are a practical resource," says Frey. "A lot of times they'll help you with their specific talents or a piece of equipment, and I've bartered and traded in that network of people throughout the city and across the country. Moreover, any chance I have to help them out, I'm going to go for it if only because I'm interested in what they're doing and want to support it."

There are many ways to keep your investments at a minimum, such as utilizing college interns for production support or sharing office space with other film professionals to split rental fees. The important thing is to track your current expenditures and plan for future goals.

"You need to understand what your costs are," advises accountant Larry Lundin. "Pay attention to the bottom line, because that will help determine your success or failure. I often see people start a business with a lot of drive, and after a year or so they lose sight of the light at the end of the tunnel and get burned out and then it's really easy to let things slip. But if you keep track of your books and watch your incoming and outgoing finances, you start to see a pattern that gives you valuable information. One of the biggest mistakes is not paying attention to costs and thinking you've got money because everyone's just paid you but you haven't really looked at your outgoing expenses."

As Larry mentioned, it is easy to neglect outgoing expenses as there may be many items you do not anticipate in your budget. In addition to production budgets for specific independent projects you intend to produce, you will need a company budget.

There are many software programs available for creating company budgets. Regardless of the program, the three major components of your budget should include most or all of the following. You many have unique items to add as well.

- ▶ *Income*
    - ▶ Estimated income (client services, film sales, and distribution)

- ▶ *Fixed Expenses*
    - ▶ Advertising
    - ▶ Annual business taxes (federal taxes, corporation fees)
    - ▶ Employee salary/benefits (if applicable)
    - ▶ Internet fees
    - ▶ Legal and professional fees (attorney, accountant, etc.)
    - ▶ Office rent and utilities (if applicable)
    - ▶ Personal monthly income from business

▶ *Estimated Regular Expenses*
  ▶ Business travel (airfare, lodging, transportation, meals)
  ▶ Car/van expenses (mileage, gas, repairs)
  ▶ Career related education (seminars, workshops)
  ▶ Equipment purchases
  ▶ Equipment repair and maintenance
  ▶ Film/video equipment rentals
  ▶ Film/video supplies (tape stock, DVDs, etc.)
  ▶ Film festivals and conferences
  ▶ Freelance support
  ▶ Office supplies and postage
  ▶ Periodicals (filmmaking magazines, directories, etc.)
  ▶ Production expenses (crews, editing, sound, talent, etc.–total the estimated expenses for all of the independent [non-funded] projects you plan to produce in the year)
  ▶ Shipping expenses
  ▶ Telephone (business)

Calculating the fixed and estimated expenses for a year will help you understand how much income is needed to stay afloat or make a profit. It will give you a barometer for ensuring that as much money is coming in as going out.

## Getting Your Name Out There

When Frey Hoffman started his company in Chicago, what he really dreamed of doing was making independent documentaries and films. He soon found, as have most of the filmmakers in this book, that that sort of creative work would not come easily, and he would have to find some other way to use his skills to support himself. He decided to try his hand at "industrial" work–that is, offering his services and equipment to commercial and corporate clients. This, he reasoned, would be a good way to enhance his skills and reputation.

However, industrial work is by no means easy to get. The jobs are limited and the competition is fierce. Frey realized he would have to work extremely hard to get his name out.

"Networking and marketing is the lifeblood of maintaining a company," says Frey of his experience in the world of industrials. "You need to find circles of people within an industry. For example, in the not-for-profit world, doing a project for one relatively well-known organization gives you the credentials to do one for another, and it's not surprising if someone at one organization knows someone at another directly. Or they know someone who knows someone else and that gives you more of a human face when you approach them. I think that's true across the board. Recently I started doing some video work for a society band and in a matter of days they referred me to another musician who wanted performances taped and edited. There's no way that second piece of work would have come without working with the first one.

"Getting involved in film organizations is also a great way to meet people. Here the local Independent Feature Project (IFP) chapter is a great resource. They run a lot of great programming and hold a conference on an annual basis. A few years back I was involved in the planning of their conference, which among many other things was definitely a positive experience in terms of meeting and working with a lot of the bastions in the Chicago film community, the Chicago Film Office, SAG, and other local producers and filmmakers."

Although Frey started with limited resources, he is making steady progress with his company, running it like the sage turtle rather than the impulsive hare. Filmmakers who are cautious about their investments, find ways to financially support themselves in the early years, and track their earnings and expenses will have a much better chance for long-term survival.

> ► CHAPTER 5

# Making Contacts: Networking and Cold Calling

*"It's amazing how so often contacts pay off years later, which is why networking needs to be an ongoing process."*

<small>JONI BRANDER, BRANDER BROADCAST CONSULTING, CHICAGO</small>

So as a new production company owner, how can you network yourself in your own community? While it is easy to look up resources on the Internet, there is nothing like the value of face-to-face communication with people who can help support your career goals or put you in touch with others who can benefit you.

In the "who you know" world of film production, networking and forming relationships to keep your company and independent projects afloat is essential. Most funding, marketing, and distribution opportunities come through referrals by mutual friends and associates.

"Networking is so key," says Jerry Vasilatos of Nitestar Productions. "It's the only way to get anything done. If you sit in your little office and put out a shingle, and even if you've paid for classified ads, you might get a couple calls a month, which isn't enough. So you've got to get out and meet people. I hate doing it. That's not to say I don't like meeting people, but there's so much BS tossed about in this business that it's very hard to sort out who is for real and who is not. But that's one of the risks you take when you go out and network. You just try to feel out who is for real and where ultimately you'll be able to team up and collaborate in a way that will be fruitful for both of you."

Networking is not just about meeting other professionals in the same field. I have received writing and production assignments from the most unlikely sources who had no connection to the film industry whatsoever. Everyone in your life should be considered part of your network, each person having their own skills, talents, and contacts that could prove useful to you, and vice versa.

Joni Brander of Brander Broadcast Consulting is one of my oldest friends. She started her company a year after I took the plunge, and we often commiserate on the many trials, triumphs, and hilarious gaffes we have made. A gifted presentation trainer, Joni is the first person I call when sweating bullets before I have to give a workshop or speech. Before I can even spout out the first sentence I intend to utter, she will say, "No, no, no. You need to redo it completely." She has taught me a lot, not only about how to give impacting presentations but also about networking. She is the queen of this disagreeable art, attending a gazillion professional and social functions every year to promote her business. She is always prodding me to attend more events to benefit my own company, knowing I have a tendency to avoid such intimidating opportunities.

"Networking needs to be an ongoing process," Joni explains. "You might not have an immediate result because a relationship may not pay off until years later. You should always be networking even if it's a purely social event, but in a very casual way where it's woven into the conversation as opposed to hammering the person over the head."

"It's very important," agrees Georgina Willis of Potoroo Films. "Kerry went to MIFF (Milan International Film Festival) a few years ago, which was the first international event she attended."

"It was good because we had done shorts at this point and we had just finished shooting our first feature, *Watermark*," says partner Kerry Rock. "I went to start talking to people about the film and about the future, knowing it was the first time I was meeting international players and financiers. I was a small fry, nobody knew who I was, but I've since met with many of those people several times. When we finished

*Watermark* it made it into Cannes. We built that link and reputation and many people that we wanted to know us now do, and that's from taking the films around and actually taking the trouble to try and meet as many people as possible."

"It is about relationships and meeting face to face," adds Georgina. "You really need to know these people and I think Kerry having gone a couple of years ago and then meeting them again every year has worked well. And it's really important to keep up correspondence. Even if a project that we've made may not be exactly what they're looking for, we'll keep in contact because we've got a diverse range of projects and maybe something else will interest them later."

## A Two-Way Street

Networking is more than just promoting yourself and your company. Building relationships is a two-way street where both parties have something to gain.

"This isn't about going out and saying I need to find someone to help me with my career," agrees Jerry Vasilatos. "I like to feel that I have something to offer because I don't want people to throw money at me and say go direct a movie if I don't think I can deliver something that actually makes their money back as well as a profit. So you have to go into networking knowing what you have to offer and trying to let other people know that and get them to believe in you."

"It certainly helps to remember you have something valuable to offer," adds Joni. "People sense when you're trying to put the big sell on them or when you're trying too hard. If you have a conversation at an event and someone is looking for something specific and you can give them a name or follow-up with some information, they usually appreciate it."

## Treat Everyone Equally

Years ago, while working at an in-house media department, I was in charge of coordinating the production interns. These poor college souls are often the brunt bearers of unwanted chores and the targets of ridicule.

I had been an intern at a television station in Providence, Rhode Island, years back where I certainly paid some dues, with much of my time spent on useless chores like typing up résumés for the producer's boyfriend. I also once fell for the age-old gag of looking for the barrel in which to empty the magnetic bulk eraser. Anyone who has been around for a few years will get that one. So having trod my own sorry path into professionalism, I treated any interns I coordinated with great respect.

Later, when I started my own company, one of my old interns was in a position to hire me as a producer/writer on various projects, which he did. Another intern went on to work at a post-production house and was able to get me free graphics for one of my independent projects. I realized that you should never, ever burn a bridge, as opportunities can come from surprising places.

"People you meet change jobs and get into positions of hiring or power, and if you've had a good relationship with people lower down the ladder that can really pay off," Joni concurs. "Every relationship counts and you never know who will refer you or who will change jobs or how careers will develop."

I also have a "what not to do" story that somehow ended with an unlikely outcome. Many years ago, while a staffer at an in-house media department, I was stressed out trying to complete an edit at a local post-production house with a tight deadline to meet. The company owner came into the edit suite and said he needed to kick me out for another client, even though I had the time booked. In my fury and exhaustion, I hurled a tape at his head. Take note—this is not a good way to build a relationship. Years later, after I had formed Amphion Productions, someone at the same post-production house hired me for a number of script projects. You can imagine my utter humiliation when I saw the company owner again. He treated me like the plague anytime I was in his facility, and I wouldn't be surprised if he warned his staff to keep me away from the tape library.

## The Intimidation Factor

Like many filmmakers in this book, I loathe schmoozing. At social or networking events I typically find myself hanging around the food table or clinging to people I already know as it feels safer than going out on a limb with a stranger. But when I do work up the nerve to chat, I realize I am putting way too much emphasis on what people do rather than who they are as individuals. Everyone you meet is a friend in the making, whether or not they can support your career goals.

A common mistake is to assume that networking will yield immediate results.

"It's good to not necessarily expect anything to happen while you're networking, as it calms you down and takes the pressure off," suggests Joni. "When I first began going to events after starting my business, I felt so much pressure to make something happen. Now I've learned to think of it more as a long-term process and that translates to me not seeming so desperate. It's easy to come across as a little too aggressive and people don't like that. If nothing happens at least you are working on relationship building. And building relationships is not necessarily talking about your business, which I think is critical to understand. Relationship building is different than the pure contact where you talk about what you do and the other person has a need for you. Those are the big hits but rare. I think your overall goal should be to know when you've left a networking event, even if you didn't get anything concrete, you were building relationships with key people. That is what's worked for me."

## The Elevator Pitch

One of Joni's tips is to develop an "elevator pitch," which is much like a screenplay logline but about your company and short enough to deliver in the time you might be with someone in an elevator.

"Have a quick pitch or line of what you do or how you can help someone at the ready and have it memorized for any situation," Joni advises. "If you're at a party, you may only get a couple minutes with a person. In the elevator pitch, it's good to talk about what you're actually doing rather than just what your title is and give an example. Instead of just saying I coach on-air talent and business executives, I could specifically say I coach anchors and reporters on their delivery and performance and executives on their presentations. If people don't have a pitch prepared they often stumble around, lose people's attention, and miss out on the opportunity. You can leave those events feeling dissatisfied and wondering if it was even worth your time."

For filmmakers, many networking opportunities arise at film festivals and media conventions, but these can be daunting experiences as there are often hordes of other filmmakers surrounding the very people you want to meet.

"At my first big convention I walked around like a big dork carrying a briefcase with brochures and quickly realized that business cards are all you really need," says Joni. "And I realized that most people who attend these types of events are open to meeting people. It helps to try to meet people early on if the festival runs for days, as by the end people are completely maxed out. You also have to work really hard to act like what you're trying to accomplish is no big deal. You have to remember the relationship side of it, talk to as many people as you can, be as relaxed as you can and know that nothing may happen immediately. It's also good to hook up with somebody in the beginning. If you go to an opening party and meet someone it helps to meet them at other events. The social aspects of these events are probably the most important for networking, as people tend to be more open and relaxed."

Once you've made your contacts, following up is critical for building ongoing relationships. This means calling or writing *more* than once.

## Taking the Chill Out of Cold-Calling

Making cold calls is a necessary evil for securing clients or seeking funds for your next film project. The thought of cold-calling puts the chill up most spines except for the most hardened sales types. Cold-calling can be especially difficult when work is slow and your self-esteem is nearing the gutter.

"Obviously there are moments of despondency when you just deposited or spent the last check that came in and you don't even have a clear idea as to where the next one will come from," says Frey Hoffman. "I think the key is to really remain focused on what is the kind of work that you're good at and like to do, and who needs that work done?

Making leads, following up those leads. That sounds deceptively simple but I think it actually is as simple as that. It's finding the gumption to make the phone calls or send the e-mails, or contact that other film-maker who's doing the same type of work and saying 'What's up?' But there are periods when you'll contact ten or fifteen people and everyone replies that there's not much going on, which can be difficult."

As uncomfortable as it feels, it is important to keep making the calls, and that's more than just once to a potential client.

"Any sales person will tell you it takes a certain number of calls to actually reach the right person, and an additional number to make a sale," says Joni. "I think when it's not your area of expertise, you tend to call once or twice and give up. Any sales person would just laugh at that. People who are not in sales also take things way too personally, while sales people take it all in stride. They know it's going to require so many calls to get a response and they know they're going to get rejected. It's a part of their day but they are relentless. Perseverance is huge, but that's where we fall short if it's not our forte. It's also something that we tend to procrastinate about. Even if you do just one hour a day of followups and making new contacts, I'm sure the payoff will come eventually."

Making cold calls sets off all kinds of immobilizing defense mechanisms. It is much easier to delay such calls by doing "busy work," because if you feel like you're accomplishing something, however minor, it justifies your procrastination. What you're really doing, of course, is protecting your fragile ego from that shattering word *No!*

The first thing you need to do, according to the experts, is acknowledge the fact that cold-calling is scary business. And by realizing and admitting that, you can begin to identify the causes of fear and address them.

Fear of cold-calling is generally brought on by a number of factors, including insecurity about your skills, the need for approval, and a poor self-image. If you analyzed those things individually, maybe you would find that you don't have that much to be afraid of after all.

## Insecurity

Although you might feel insecure about your production skills, chances are you know what you're doing. You may just be intimidated by the competition. There's a term in sales called "positioning." If you try to position yourself as number one in the industry, then that perception might become a reality. But to position yourself as number one, you do need to be able to offer your prospective clients the kind of valuable services that they need by staying abreast of the trends and technology and sharpening your skills on an on-going basis. You need to ask questions to find out what problems your clients are facing and how you can help overcome them.

## The Need for Approval

From childhood, to dating, to the workplace, the need for approval is paramount for all of us. It's part of being human and something that is taught and reinforced throughout our lives by methods of punishment versus reward.

When faced with a cold call, the chance of getting approval from a total stranger whose busy day you are interrupting is pretty slim. Most unpracticed cold callers expect hostile rejection. But rather than try to change the behavior of the people you call (I'll call so-and-so because I gave her friend a referral so I know she'll be nice to me), you probably need to change your expectations.

Rarely will you run into a fire-breathing dragon on the other end of the line. And if you do, it won't ruin your career. You should instead expect a neutral response, which is the most likely situation you'll face. Indifference is not rejection. It is a normal reaction from a preoccupied stranger and not a personal affront against you.

A technique psychologists use to help patients deal with their phobias is paradoxical intention. This might be the method for you if you are terrified of making cold calls. Paradoxical intention means conjuring up extreme images of what you fear. Imagine the worst possible thing that could happen when you make a call. For example, you might imagine that the person at the other end of the line screams at you for ruining his day. He tells you that you are a worthless filmmaker and should never hope to get a project from him or anyone else in town. He tells you that if he ever sets eyes on you, he will personally rip your head off for being so impudent as to call while he's working at a *real* job. Ridiculous, huh? The absurdity of such an image helps to deflate fear by exposing it for what it really is, not what your imagination can frighten you into believing it is. It is hard for the human mind to accept both the fear and the absurd image you have put in your consciousness. And if you can face the possibility of being screamed at and threatened, then anything a potential client might say on the phone surely couldn't be as bad.

### Self-Image

It is also important to remember that you can't change another person's behavior. If someone doesn't buy into what you're offering, you shouldn't feel inadequate. False expectations like that will slowly erode your self-image. Remember, your film production company is as legitimate as their business. You are a professional too, and you have something valuable to offer. If circumstances prevent them from taking advantage of it now, opportunities may still exist down the road.

Cold-calling is a gamble, a Russian roulette of sorts, but a key to success is in the understanding that security comes from within. It comes from the knowledge that you are good at what you do, and from the belief that you *can* hurdle obstacles that block your path.

### Cold-Calling Tips

- ▶ Pre-plan what you are going to say.
- ▶ Arrange for privacy so you won't be interrupted.
- ▶ Put everything else aside to focus on making the calls.
- ▶ Use a tracking system to keep a record of the person's name, number, and date you talked, so when you follow up, you have a record of previous conversations.
- ▶ If there are objections or concerns, re-focus your prospective client.
- ▶ End with a firm next step, such as "May I send you a company brochure?" or "I'll be in touch next month to see if any new projects have come up."
- ▶ Practice cold-calling by role-playing to uncover and deal with any objections you may hear.

## Taking Advantage of Slow Times

Fortunately, or unfortunately, in spite of all the contacts that you make, there will be times when the work just cannot be conjured up. However, Joni insists that they are really necessary to any business.

"Slow times really give you a chance to do all those things you push aside, like accounting or updating your Web site," says Joni. "There's always so much to do. You're not getting paid for it but the slow times are essential because if you were always just doing the main part of your business you'd never have time to work on those other tasks that are so easy to put off. And when you have a tenure of ten or twelve years you can look back and say it's always slow in January. But when you first start out and have nothing to go on, you wonder, should I even be doing this? Is this a sign? Without a track record to 'look at, the panic attacks are' even worse."

But slow times can provide an opportunity to jumpstart your own creative projects. "During a down time I got my documentary project *Metaphysical Dice* going," says Frey. "I got in touch with a friend who does camera and sound work for television and industrials, and we'd talked about doing something on our own. I pitched him on the idea and then we went out on the streets of Chicago and asked people three questions. One, do they believe in destiny? Two, depending on how they answered that, did they feel like their vision of destiny was apropos to the world at large beyond their personal lives, and three, if they had a chance to roll a pair of dice that would put them in another person's life throughout time or history or immediately to another place in the city, would they roll the dice?"

When my own work ground to a screeching halt after 9/11, I took the time to produce three documentaries on people with disabilities, part of the "Broken Wings" series now being distributed by Chip Taylor Communications. Had I been swamped with work, chances are that I would not have completed these personally important projects.

"It's absolutely normal to have slow times in business. Even big corporate America has slow times," says Joni. "It was something I hadn't really thought about until I had my own business because you still had to turn up for work every day."

If you have the discipline to work every day, even when times are slow and no boss is holding a paycheck over your head, if you have the gumption to face putting yourself out there, and if you are resourceful enough to make the best of difficult times, you are on your way toward fulfilling your dreams.

# CHAPTER 6

# Funding Opportunities for Filmmakers

*"Obviously you were put here to make these art pieces for us. Always know that you are loved for that."*

CAROLE DEAN, FROM THE HEART PRODUCTIONS, OXNARD, CA

Creative filmmakers and documentary makers often rely on grants and other sources of funding for their projects. Many grants require nonprofit status. It is hard to survive as a nonprofit, so some production companies develop nonprofit subsidiaries in order to qualify for grants. For example, Leslie Kussman of Aquarius Productions in Medfield, Massachusetts, created Solstice Films, an organization separate from her for-profit company that allows her to qualify as a nonprofit for documentary grants.

Fortunately, nonprofit status isn't always necessary and many other funding opportunities exist for filmmakers.

One such funding source is presided over by Carole Dean—the Roy W. Dean Grants, an in-kind services grant for film and documentary makers from around the globe, so named to honor her late father. In addition to supervising the grant and running her production company, Carole is author of *The Art of Funding Your Film* and hosts many workshops on the topic. She is the ultimate guru on chasing dollars to finance productions.

When I spoke to Carole she was in New Zealand, a place she frequents often to support filmmakers and screenwriters through her grant offerings. Warm, spiritual, and compassionate, her advice is always encouraging and positive. Through her research she has discovered that there is more money than ever available for filmmakers, despite the myths or uncertain economic trends.

"When you hear that some division of government or an arts group has cut its funding, that can cause a very negative perception," warns Carole. "And yet I would say that every time that happens, at the same time there are three, four, or dozens of new companies starting up that have grants available. It may not be as easy to get $100,000 or $50,000 from one place anymore, but you can get the $5,000 and $10,000 grants from a lot of small places. You need to be realistic about how much time it's going to take to get your funding and that means allowing yourself several months for research. In my book I listed one search engine with ten thousand funding places. Think how much time it would take you to get through that alone! It's the work you need to do to find those $5,000 to $10,000 grants that's time consuming."

Before you start seeking the dollars for your dream project, here's what Carole says you should always do.

"I really recommend that filmmakers do an outline that says they're going to raise X dollars. And I suggest they break their project into three sections–pre-production and research, production, and post. At the beginning you really need to focus on the first third. How much money do you need and when do you need it by? You have to have a mindset with total faith. You cannot carry baggage around in your mind when looking for money or when planning your production needs. You have to be totally confident and realistic."

Carole has reviewed thousands of proposals for the Roy W. Dean grants so she has an eye for what differentiates those she is interested in supporting.

"I like to look at a photo of the filmmaker while I read the proposal," says Carole. "Not necessarily a photo of you with a camera on your shoulder, but just of a picture of who you are so we can see a look in your eyes that tells us how committed you are to spending three years to make this film. Secondly, what is your connection to this film? If you're working on an Alzheimer's project, did your grandfather have Alzheimer's? If you have found a man whose life you want to document, what's so special about the man and why are you the one that needs to tell the story? Answering those questions at the front of your application will allow your funder to know why you are willing to devote so much time to the project. Your personal drive for telling the story is really the basis of the film, so it needs to be explained early on.

"Another thing is that filmmakers get so involved in the technology—I'm going to shoot on this or that camera and they forget that filmmakers are storytellers. I want to know the story. Don't forget that part. And in telling me your story, I want visuals. I want you to relate the story in a way I can visualize it on film. In my book I had some examples about taking a statement, such as 'seventy-six thousand Americans lost their lives in World War II.' Turn that around into 'these soldiers are now lying in shallow, make-shift graves, rusting wrecks and battlefields thousands of miles from home' and you provide the images we need to follow your vision."

## The Film Proposal

There are many books and Internet resources on creating proposals for film projects but a common mistake is to submit a "final" proposal carte blanche to a variety of funding sources without paying attention to application guidelines. Each funding source is looking for specific information they want to see addressed, so time must be given to alter and adhere your proposal to meet these guidelines.

"You'd be surprised how many people send me proposals and say 'I'm going to send this to fifty granters,' " says Carole. "I say 'No, no, don't do that! You have to read the Web sites.' The worst thing that a person applying for a grant can do is not read the guidelines because it means that you're in a hurry, you don't want to take the time, or you're not focused. Granters know when you've not read their guidelines."

While it takes time to tailor a proposal to each specific granter or sponsor, it is important to search for multiple opportunities rather than pin your hopes in one place. Hundreds, if not thousands, of filmmakers may apply for the same grant, so there is a strong likelihood of rejection, especially with the larger funding sources. Rejection is not a sign of failure but a chance to learn and improve, especially if the funding source provides feedback, as many do. Carole Dean personally telephones Roy W. Dean grant applicants who have not made the final cut. I've had a few such calls from Carole myself and felt more uplifted than deterred as a result, as she acknowledged the relevance of my projects while offering constructive suggestions for improvement.

"I have never sent letters," says Carole. "I'll admit sometimes it takes a bottle of wine to make those phone calls because I get so emotional and I always feel so bad about having to say no. I'll set aside two weeks and two to three hours a day to take phone calls. I will go over the application with the filmmakers and give them a private consultation on how to improve their application. I feel if we're going to say no, we should darned sure explain why we said no or what a film-maker can do to improve it."

Although proposals vary depending on funding guidelines, there are some general components that are typically included:

1. Story synopsis
2. Program structure and style (the creative approach)
3. Relevance of the project (why this story needs to be told)
4. Production budget
5. Plans for marketing and distribution
6. The production team (bios on the key players)
7. Pertinent articles or resources (supporting the relevance of the project)
8. Contact information

For example, the following is a proposal for a documentary I created called *Touched by a Mentor*, about the importance of mentoring for youth. This proposal was chosen as a finalist in the 2003 Roy W. Dean LA Video Grant. For this submission, a budget was not required so is not included in the sample. As Carole suggested, always read the funding guidelines and follow them!

PROPOSAL SAMPLE

# TOUCHED BY A MENTOR

*Producer/Writer: Sara Caldwell, Amphion Productions*

## Synopsis

For those brave enough to seek a better life and for those caring enough to "give back," one common ground is Cabrini Connections, a nationally recognized youth program in Chicago. Here, nearly 100 inner-city teens find a new focus off the streets through one-on-one mentoring.

*Touched by a Mentor* is a one-hour documentary that will profile student/mentor pairs at Cabrini Connections to explore the power and importance of such relationships to economically disadvantaged youth. In addition to witnessing the tenuous but tight bonds that form between often distrustful teens and caring adults, we will also find out about Cabrini Connections, including the program's unique methodology for encouraging mentor/student relationships to continue from school through career and the incredible work and dedication of staff and volunteers who provide the impetus for the program's success.

Larry Lapidus, Lapidus Photography.

The documentary will be hosted by Isaiah Brooms, a former student in the program who will bring a unique and personal perspective on how mentoring gave him a bridge to new worlds of opportunity. He will host the program in the Cabrini Green Housing District where he grew up. Despite difficult circumstances, Isaiah's involvement in tutoring programs enabled him to get college scholarships and he graduated with degrees in theater and education from

Bradley University in Peoria, IL. (*A sample clip of Isaiah is provided in this packet*)

As the program unfolds, audiences will become more vested in the success of the student/mentor relationships, which will undoubtedly be besieged by challenges from home, work, school, peer pressure, self-doubt, gang hostility, and numerous other prevalent issues faced by youth in poverty. It is impossible to predict how the profiled relationships will be impacted by such issues, but chances are the students' involvement in Cabrini Connections and the special relationships they forge with their mentors will have a profound impact on how they respond to them. Isaiah and other former students will lend their voices on how mentor relationships affected their lives.

## About Cabrini Connections

*Cabrini Connections*, a grass-roots nonprofit organization, is not an ordinary after-school program. In addition to a highly successful track record of getting hundreds of adults and youth connected in non-school tutor/mentor programs, it is also an extraordinary model of excellence. Headed by CEO Daniel Bassill, a twenty-eight-year veteran of leading tutor/mentor programs, the organization has created a comprehensive database and maps of Chicago that visually show the distribution of existing programs and where there are voids in areas of poverty and poorly performing schools. The organization also helps new or existing programs succeed through a vast offering of resources and support systems, such as interactive Web sites and biannual training and leadership conferences for tutoring staff and volunteers. These services are offered with the goal of gathering and organizing all that is known about successful non-school tutor/mentor programs and sharing that knowledge to expand the availability and enhance the effectiveness of these services to children throughout Chicago and any poverty area of the country.

*Touched by a Mentor* will showcase the personal experiences of the profiled mentors and students within the context of Cabrini Connections' philosophies and strategies, wide-ranging ones that involve participation from schools, businesses, volunteers, city officials, and other important stakeholders in our youth's success.

(*Detailed information on Cabrini Connections can be found at www.tutormentorconnection.org.*)

## Program Style

Scenes in the teens' home, school, and "street" life will be shot with a gritty, urban reality. At the same time, the overall theme of the piece is one of hope and caring, so positive messages and imagery about the power of student/mentor relationships will be reinforced throughout.

## How *Touched by a Mentor* Will Benefit Society

Today more than ever, audiences need programs that enlighten and inspire; programs that provide a greater understanding of the human condition and the ways in which we are all inextricably linked, regardless of race, age, or gender. *Touched by a Mentor* reveals many such links as tutors and students learn about each other and realize that they do, indeed, have a lot in common. As they accept this, the mentors become strong role models of caring and success. In turn, the students' willingness to rise above negative surroundings and expectations instills feelings of hope and purpose for the mentors. By showcasing these very personal and fascinating stories, *Touched by a Mentor* has the power to inspire, educate, and provide long-term solutions for youth in poverty.

## Plans for Distribution

Amphion Productions is in the early stages of developing a Web site to encourage the sharing of stories, link interchanges, and resources related to tutor/mentoring, which will be linked to and promoted by Cabrini Connections. Cabrini Connections will also encourage its sponsors to financially contribute to the project. The program will be offered to PBS and other cable networks and will be entered into appropriate film festivals.

*Touched by a Mentor* can have a tremendous educational value so distribution in the educational marketplace would be sought immediately. Since more than 50 percent of the videos purchased by this nation's 6,000 libraries are non-theatrical, non-theatrical school and library distributors will be contracted to promote the documentary to educational markets. In addition, the program will be offered to reviewers of educational media such as Booklists, Video Librarian, Video Rating Guide and others.

### The Production Team

*Producer/Writer*: The producer/writer of the documentary is Sara Caldwell of Amphion Productions in the Los Angeles area. Since forming Amphion Productions in 1991, Sara has worked on over 150 film, documentary, and other media programs and can pull professional crews and services from a wide talent pool. She has worked as an episode writer/producer for the **Discovery Health Channel** series "Medical Diary," is the co-producer, writer, and director for a new television series on people with disabilities called *Broken Wings*, and the producer/writer of a WTTW (PBS) documentary on impoverished children called *Cabrini Green . . . what you don't see*. Sara is also co-author of *So You Want to be a Screenwriter: How to Face the Fears and Take the Risks* (Allworth Press) and conducts numerous screenwriting workshops around the country from which she donates 50 percent of registration fees to nonprofit organizations.

Sara has a great passion for telling stories with social value that reflect a wide range of human experiences. She was inspired to develop this documentary from her own experiences. She began mentoring in 1989 and is still in close contact with her student, Isaiah Brooms, who will host this project. Sara was one of the original founders and a past board director of Cabrini Connections. She currently serves the organization in an advisory capacity and helps with fundraising and other activities. Sara has also been a volunteer/fundraiser for homeless shelters, disability organizations, and women in prison.

*(For more information, please visit Sara's company website at www.amphionpro.com)*

**Post-Production**: Jerry Vasilatos of Nitestar Pro-ductions in Los Angeles will complete post-production on ***Touched by a Mentor*** on his Avid MC Express Elite editing system. Jerry was the co-producer and editor of *A Refuge and Me*, which documents the life of a Burmese refugee and his quest to obtain an illegal Thai identification card in order to aid his refugee family living along the border. Jerry wrote, produced, directed, and edited the independent holiday drama *Solstice*, broadcast nationally as a Lifetime Television Original World Premier Movie and recognized with silver and bronze awards in the Charleston and Houston International Film Festivals, respectively. Jerry has edited numerous independent films, documentaries, and trailers and is very familiar with and supportive of Cabrini Connections. *(www.nitestar.com)*

**Production Assistance**: Students from Cabrini Connections' Innervision Youth Productions (IYP) will be paid interns and will have the opportunity for hands-on training with a professional crew.

IYP is in its seventh year of offering a video club to students enrolled in Cabrini Connections. IYP encourages and teaches students to produce short videos in a manner that entertains, educates, and motivates the viewers to become active supporters of tutor/mentor programs throughout the Chicago region. The videos allow the students to express their creativity, build self-esteem, and acquire critical thinking skills to deal with issues in their own lives. IYP is led by a team of production professionals and college students studying film and video. The annual IYP film festival is held every March and is shown to an audience of more than 100.

*Other crew to be determined.*

**Contact Us**

For more information on **Touched by a Mentor**, please contact Sara Caldwell at (661) 260-1135 or amphionpro@ yahoo.com.

## The Pitch

Equally important to a powerful, visual proposal is the "pitch." The pitch is how you orally describe your project in a few minutes to a prospective funder. Carole likens the pitch to a baseball game.

"Many times you think the pitcher knows what he's doing, but if you watch carefully, it's the catcher who's telling the pitcher what to pitch. Even though you may have your pitch set, you need to know who your catcher is, and that would be your funder or your investor. If you're talking to a man who's got money but is wearing a twenty-year old pair of shoes or a ten-year old suit, you know that this is a conservative person so you'll be very conservative in your presentation of your film and speak accordingly. Paying attention to who you're talking to is number one. Secondly, the delivery of the pitch is the paramount key. It should never be longer than three minutes and if it is a story with names, you need to provide the names at the beginning so investors knew who the hero or heroine is. In other words, who are we rooting for? Thirdly, you tell the story. Again, this is storytelling. We don't care what camera you're going to shoot with. That's not important in the pitch. The pitch has got to reach out and grab someone's heart. It has to elevate them enough to want to open their checkbook and be part of your organization."

In her book, Carole provides four ideas for developing the perfect pitch to present to a foundation.

1. List three compelling reasons why this film should be made.
2. Describe your connection to the story and explain why you are the one who should make this film.
3. Who will benefit from this film?
4. What is the urgency?

Carole also advises honesty about the risks involved for investors.

"No matter what your pitch is, in addition to telling them what you expect to make back you should let them know that film is a risky business and nothing is guaranteed."

## Fundraising

Filmmakers are creative, so it is no wonder we hear intriguing fundraising stories on a regular basis, from the person who maxes out his credit cards (not recommended) to someone who tours the country in a rock band to raise money in ticket sales. I once met a filmmaker who attended festivals in a Godzilla-like costume to try to secure backing for his creature-from-the-sea feature. Another drove around in a "film mobile" with a loudspeaker and a huge sign that read "Help me make my movie!"

Film funding can be obtained in countless ways, from begging Mom and Dad to approaching gargantuan studios and corporations. In addition to foundations and grants, some popular tactics include hosting fundraising house parties, getting private investments through individuals and businesses, distribution presales (also known as gap financing), secured or unsecured loans, selling ancillary rights (such as the soundtrack), and product placement.

"That is one area that is underdeveloped in part," says Carole, of product placement and branding. "Where we're going now is what they call convergence, especially in television. That means that you're going to find the Coca-Colas when you open a fridge, so you're going to associate Coke with the Johnson family as the Coke will be on the set somewhere every week. The same with cereals and all kinds of products. These days, people zap out commercials, using remotes and other, more sophisticated electronic devices, so the commercial people are thinking far ahead, and they're going to start putting their products inside productions more and more, which is very good for independent filmmakers. Another thing that filmmakers can do in addition to sending their script and proposal to the larger product placement companies, like Aim Productions in New York and Feature This! in California, is to look at their scripts and see what locations or props are needed. For example, if you need a restaurant to shoot in, that might cost you eight to ten thousand dollars a day. But if a restaurant owner likes your story and sees the promotional aspects, you might get that location for free or even get food for the crew. This is a creative way to save money on your production."

## The Filmmaker's Journey

The filmmaking process is long, arduous, and uncertain, but the more you can visualize the end of the journey, the easier it will be to head in the right direction. Carole describes the process as a road trip.

"If you were going on a trip somewhere you would certainly know your final destination, and the same thing applies to filmmakers. Filmmakers get so excited about their project but can get lost in the detail of making it happen so they're not always focused on the end goal. One of the first things you need ask yourself is where does this film belong? On HBO? Discovery Channel? Court TV? Then you know exactly how you want your film to run and what you want to do with it. I think that to materialize the film you need to visualize the film screening and see your name on the screen, the director's name, and editor's name, and see that with a lot of emotion and belief and feel the success and the pride. If you can visualize the audience, you can visualize the potential funders."

Any filmmaker who has not applied for a Roy W. Dean grant, one of the largest independent film grants in the United States, should certainly consider the option by visiting *www.fromtheheartproductions.com*. Carole's book, *The Art of Funding Your Film*, is also an invaluable and comprehensive resource. Her wisdom, experience, focus, and compassion have resulted in her own success. Applying these same traits to your filmmaking career will only boost it.

"Always remember that your mind is your most powerful tool," concludes Carole. "Use your mind to create your art and manifest the money, contacts, and the right people to your project, and always maintain yourself in the highest caliber. Keep your mind free of resentment and negativity. Live with thoughts of forgiveness and love and acceptance and enjoy what you're doing."

▶ **PART II**

# INVESTING IN YOURSELF

# CHAPTER 7

# Working with Investors—What's in It for Them?

*"Most people don't understand that filmmaking is a business and like any business it's got rules."*

MICHAEL HARPSTER, MARKETING & DISTRIBUTION EXPERT, LOS ANGELES

When filmmakers do not have the financial means to produce their independent projects, they often seek investors. The first thing investors will care about is the profitability of the film. Films do not need to be high budget or "Hollywood" style to capture investors' attention, ergo successes like *Hoop Dreams, My Big Fat Greek Wedding,* and *The Blair Witch Project.* When a filmmaker and investor can work well together, the need for Hollywood is greatly reduced. But the harsh reality is that most independent films never show a financial return on investment.

Michael Harpster is a thirty-year veteran of the film industry since starting his career with New Line Cinema in 1970. He was president of marketing at New Line for ten years and executive producer for three of the company's pictures. In 1999 he became president of marketing for Providence and is currently overseeing distribution for Constellation and Caliente Entertainment. Nobody knows film investment and marketing better, although he offers some bitter pills to swallow.

"I would say 90 to 95 percent of individuals who get into the film business lose all their money. There are many reasons for that. Mainly people don't think of film as a business. They approach it for non-financial reasons, which are usually ideological or emotional. That doesn't mean people can't find investors. There were over two thousand pictures trying to get into Sundance last year and the money for those films came from somewhere, though mostly as a combination of family and credit cards. But that Mom and Pop investment business rarely pays off. Maybe one film a year gets sold for big money and perhaps five films get decent distribution. There are ways for private investors to profit in the film business but it's generally not on a one-time basis, which of course is exactly what the filmmakers want because their project is so wonderful. Nine times out of ten it's a total piece of sh*t without any marketing plans or marketability so everybody suffers."

Today there are a host of Web sites and consultants that help link filmmakers with investors, but typically investors are acquired through careful research, intense networking, and having the guts to knock down doors. Not surprisingly, many business types (left-brain thinkers) are intrigued about the prospect of getting involved in a creative endeavor but for them to have confidence in your film, they need to see *your* confidence in being able to carry the project through to completion, all the way to distribution. Spouting wimpy, nonspecific slogans like "We're sure this will be shown at Sundance" or "The film will do great in foreign markets" will unlikely yield positive results.

## Working with Investors

You should never raise funds or negotiate contracts without seeking good legal advice, as there are many intricacies involved. For example, if you make an offering to a private investor you need to supply a "private placement memoranda," which contains information required by state and federal securities laws. Without including these disclosures, which often change year to year, a filmmaker can be held personally liable. Also, keep in mind that an entertainment attorney's job is not just to coordinate the paperwork but also to assist in negotiations.

Of course, your company must be a legal entity in order to raise funds, such as a limited partnership or corporation.

## Private Investments

Private investments are the most typical way in which low-budget films (under $3 million) get made. A private investor might be a banker or your wealthy Aunt Martha. Private investments involve many securities and contractual laws, no matter who you are dealing with, so it is imperative to have good legal counsel. It is also important to disclose the inherent risky business aspects of investing in a film project.

In most states, securities laws limit you to twenty-five private investors without having to make complicated SEC filings and declarations. Investors must also be updated on the progress of your film and allowed to see financial records.

## Studios

Most films financed by studios have the best success for funding and distribution. Studios typically offer an up-front fee for the film in exchange for a hefty percentage. Major studios also typically manage their own promotion and distribution. However, studio deals are very difficult to come by, especially for unknown filmmakers or those out of the mainstream.

## Independent Production Companies

There are a number of independent production companies who have studio deals to produce a certain number of projects. While most of these projects are produced "in-house," a few are typically "outsourced." Again, getting these types of deals is difficult (though not impossible) for filmmakers without established reputations.

## Foreign Financing

Some countries offer tax incentives to encourage a film industry to develop, though typically involve only partial financing. Some of the trade-offs might be requirements to hire local crews, talent, and production/post facilities.

## Pre-Distribution Deals

Distribution deals can be negotiated before, during, or after production. Although most deals occur after a film is completed, some distributors offer an advance that can help cover production or finishing costs. (See chapter 19 for more detailed information about working with distributors.)

## Brokers and Loans

All too many filmmakers are tempted and seduced by brokers who essentially operate like credit card companies by finding loans with high interest rates. Most lenders require collateral and have stringent repayment periods. If you have arrived here as a "last resort" you may want to question the validity of your project, assuming all other funding sources have rejected it.

## What's in It for the Investor?

If you put yourself in the investor's shoes, what would you gain from supporting your particular film project, financially and personally? When Rob Hardison of Rainforest Films needed money for his second feature, *Trois*, he approached the local African-American business community for help. He knew this was the best pool to support a film made by and starring African Americans, and he secured 100 percent of his financing from that community.

After filmmaker Brad Sykes of Nightfall Pictures in Los Angeles had acquired 50 percent of his funding for a horror feature, he approached a horror film distributor he had previously worked with to secure the other 50 percent. The connection is obvious. The more you can connect your investors to your project on a personal or business level, the more likely they will write that check you so desperately need.

Investors also want to see integrity, honesty, and a track history of your experience as a filmmaker. Parlaying your project through smoke and mirrors may have an initial impact but could hurt you in the long run. Being honest about the high-risk realities of investing in a film project will earn an investor's respect, as long as it is built around heartfelt enthusiasm and well-researched information on the marketing and distribution potential.

"I truly believe that filmmakers must be dead honest with everyone about what's going on," says Carole Dean. "Honesty and integrity pay off. Anytime you make a financial deal with someone, it must be of the highest caliber, in that it must make money for all involved. We're in the film *business* and there most be something profitable for each person involved, or don't make the deal."

It is only natural for investors to have concerns and questions such as, what stage is the film currently in and when will it be finished? Who is going to distribute the project domestically and internationally? Who is attached as talent?

The amount of money that an investor puts into a film varies widely depending on the size of the budget, the country of origin, and so forth. Investors are typically offered anywhere from 5 to 20 percent of profits, although this also varies dramatically from project to project. As investors only see a return on profits, they have to wait a very long time between putting money down at the onset of a production to seeing that return, if any, at distribution. Obviously, film investment is a long-term gamble.

Michael Harpster has shared sensible advice in numerous articles targeted to individuals considering an investment in films. His advice to potential investors is sobering to hear, for both those who aspire to invest and those who aspire to be invested in:

"Don't put up more than 50 percent for one project; spread your money over ten projects or more," he cautions investors. "Make sure the distribution is in place, and that it makes sense to you. Understand how to run the numbers. If the film doesn't yield at least 50 percent of its budget from foreign revenues, you can kiss it goodbye. It will never make any money because it puts way too much of the recovery on the domestic side, which is the toughest side."

"Filmmakers," he says, have a tendency to "see the money, pounce on it, and overwhelm the investor, because all they're thinking about is the picture." He cautions them to understand that investors are usually looking for the longevity of a filmmaker, not a one-time, hit-or-miss project.

"Filmmakers need to think more about the process and less about the project. Once you bring an investor into the process then you can make good decisions about the project related to the process. It's true you should have a lead project to sell or start a portfolio with but that can also lead you down the wrong alley. Let's say an investor wants to drill oil wells. You don't just drill one well. You have to drill a bunch because what are the chances that the one you drill is going to bubble with oil? Very, very small. Filmmaking is the same. Of all those people that submit one film to Sundance, 98 percent of them will never make another."

Michael reiterated what so many filmmakers in this book have stated, and that is the importance of having multiple projects, or oil drills, in various stages of development.

## Approaching Investors

Approaching potential investors is scary business, and doing it prematurely is a common mistake. The closer you are to having your film ready to go (i.e., you have already attached a good director, director of photography, and talent, have secured all of your locations, and hopefully a distribution deal in writing) the easier it will be for you to entice investors as it appears you will go forward with or without their help. You will need exactly the same kind of pitch and proposal for a private investor as you would for a nonprofit funder or granter; see the previous chapter.

Investors need to know at the offset that filmmaking is a gamble so your proposal should include a risk statement. An investor may be an entrepreneur willing to take a high level of financial risk if he or she believes in your project, the quality of the script, and the director and talent but of course does not want to simply throw money away. Having a realistic, reasonable budget and a marketing and distribution plan are keys to enticing investors. Well-researched comparisons to other films in the same budget and genre can also be a useful tool, as long as the comparisons are realistic.

"One of the biggest problems of independent films in general is that they look toward what the majors are doing as something achievable for them and that's simply not the case," says Michael. "I wish that filmmakers who talk investors into this business would really look at their numbers and take a responsibility. Most of them do not. The business is fairly predictable because now through things like IMBD and some of the other databases, you can see the television revenue and look at the business cycle of virtually any film that you care to. But most people don't do that with diligence. Most investors don't and certainly most filmmakers don't want to do that because they're afraid what they'll do is point out that it's not going to work."

As Michael suggested, waffling about projections for potential domestic and international sales by comparing your film to the majors is not what's going to convince an investor. Rather, you need to show the financial results of independent films that share the same style and budget that you are planning.

*www.the-numbers.com* is an excellent resource for looking up budgets versus gross revenues. For example, you can see that a film like *Swingers* had a production budget of $200,000 and a print and advertising budget of $700,000. To date, the film has enjoyed a U.S. gross of $4,505,992 and a worldwide gross of $6,542,637, making it one of the twenty most profitable movies ever made based on return of investment. Not surprisingly, *The Blair Witch Project* tops the list as of this writing.

On the flipside, you can see the multitude of biggest money losers, again based on return of investment. This list includes some hefty production budgets where a return was questionable to begin with. One of the lower budget projects is Barry Levinson's 2000 would-be comedy, *An Everlasting Piece*. The film cost $4,000,000 but only recouped $75,078 by 2004. Someone lost a bundle on that one.

For independent filmmakers, small budgets are certainly easier to raise and offer better prospects for making a profit. Providing your investors with a realistic budget and revenue potential is vital.

## Control Issues

Many filmmakers in this book have chosen not to use investors for one simple reason—giving up creative control. Oftentimes investors, who may have little experience in film production, want to have a say during the production and editing phases. This can lead to conflicts between the investor and filmmaker.

"I spent a year constantly arguing with financiers about their creative input into the script, and it's a really dangerous and scary thing because they give you money and will expect to have a say," says Ruba Nadda of Coldwater Productions. "Some people have good ideas that you can use, but other times they come to you with insane suggestions. Filmmakers need to pick their battles and make sure they know their story. It's really easy to tear up the arguments if you stick to the core of what your movie's about."

An investor's role during production can be written into the proposal and contracts, but tact and consideration should be taken for those offering large financial commitments. Carole Dean suggests discussing such investor and filmmaker roles at the beginning of the process.

"When the funder comes in, you say to them, 'You're invited to every meeting on this film that you would like to come to. You wouldn't be a participant, you would be there to watch and listen and enjoy the process. And if you have ideas and suggestions, you're very welcome to come to me afterward and give them. If they work for us, we might use them.' It's very important that all agreements are clarified ahead of time to prevent any unhappiness during the process of filming because there's only one producer and one director, and that has to be clear from the beginning."

## Investors versus Self-Financing

Another reason filmmakers choose not to use investors is when they can produce their projects with very minimal funding. If so, why complicate matters and potentially lose creative control?

"I do a radio talk show and often interview filmmakers who have spent thousands of dollars on their projects," says Les Szeleky of Secret's Out Productions and host of the B+ Movie Making radio show on Adren-alineRadio.com. "They have friends or family with a lot of money or they went out and got investors. Whenever I hear that somebody got down on both knees to raise money for a film, I think they're awesome. Being able to raise thousands of dollars from other people just blows me away. I'm not a fundraiser by any stretch of the imagination and I've never been able to find funding. *Vampire Time Travelers* was the most expensive movie I've made and I did something I will never, ever do again and I completely discourage others from doing it. I financed the project on credit cards but there's a thing called finance charge and darn it, it's compounded! Hello! I learned that the hard way. The good news is that it was still very inexpensive. There are filmmakers charging $100,000 on credit cards and that's absolutely insane. Except for that one case, I make movies for literally nothing. I'm not kidding. Some people say they spent $10,000 as if that's not much. I spend nothing and I mean *nothing*. Ten years ago, before digital technology, there was an excuse for not being able to make movies. Now if you're not out making a movie, the number one reason is that you just don't want to make it. It's not exciting enough to you because if it was, you'd be out there doing it."

While raising funds for a film project may seem overwhelming, it is not necessary to do it alone. Being in a partnership can benefit the process tremendously. For example, if you're planning to direct your own project, a producer can be invaluable in concentrating on the funding, budgeting, and business aspects. Such a partnership may mean sharing co-ownership of a project, but a team approach that combines specific business and creative skills tends to reap the best results. Looking at alternative markets can also have some advantages.

"A place where people can make money is to get something on DVD or video that has marketability" says Michael Harpster. "There is a lot of money being made in that area right now, which will continue over the next few years. These will generally not be features as much as special interest programming, like skateboard or fitness movies. The economics of DVDs are tremendously attractive to investors as you don't have to spend one or two million in production. You can spend between $20,000 to $100,000 and slap it into a DVD. If you can sell 20,000 units on a Web site, you're home free."

There are pros and cons to working with investors but if you decide to pursue this route, honesty, integrity, thoughtful research, planning, and enthusiasm are tantamount. Also, learn how to play by the rules.

"There are rules for an investor and independent producer," says Michael. "It's not difficult to understand. It took me about fifteen years but I'm kind of a slow learner."

# CHAPTER 8

# Makin' Movies Y'all

*"If you can find a way to put rims on your car, some gold teeth in your mouth and get that new polo t-shirt, then you can find a way to shoot your own movie."*

ROB HARDY, RAINFOREST FILMS, MARIETTA, GA

**A**s challenging as movie making is, imagine that you are an engineering college student with no experience in screenwriting or film production, there is no film department on campus, and you have never seen a film camera in your life. What are your chances of getting a feature project off the ground?

## Chocolate City

Despite a lack of experience, resources, and contacts, Florida A&M students Rob Hardy and William (Will) Packer shattered the Hollywood myths to produce a feature film. In the early 1990s these students produced and directed *Chocolate City*, a story about the struggles of a young man trying to define himself at a historically Black college. The feature was made on a budget of $20,000 and released nationally to home video and distributed independently over the Internet. After completing their first feature, Rob and Will went on to form Marietta-based Rainforest Films and produce a string of successful movies. While *Chocolate City* didn't generate a substantial return, the exposure and experience paved the way for more fruitful projects.

Rob Hardy recalls the early challenges of trying to get *Chocolate City* off the ground.

"I wanted to be a filmmaker but I was majoring in something else and my school didn't have a film program. I spent the summer trying to land a film or television internship but nobody accepted me. So I wrote a treatment, which later became a screenplay and galvanized some other students to try to make the film happen. We also got together with some students at nearby Florida State University, developed a list of equipment that we'd need, and began raising money. We did a lot of fundraising and because we were at a state-funded school, we could get people to donate things as a tax deduction. We also got money from on-campus organizations and, as a result, we were able to do all of our casting and crew selections. Our director of photography, ACs, and script supervisors came from the Florida State film department but the rest were non-trained A&M students.

"We began shooting our film with no real concept of what it meant to have a real story structure. We had no concept of character development or first, second, and third acts. I learned that all on the fly. I knew a lot of people who did music, so we pulled our musical resources in and developed a soundtrack and score. After the shoot we had to get the film processed and cut so we went out and raised more money for that. A local video company that produced the sports show for our football team donated their editing bay. We used a linear, and I underscore *linear*, editing system to do the rough cut. With non-digital linear editing, you have to put in one tape, then a second tape, and then flip the switch to do your manual dissolve and it outputs the scene to a third tape with a certain amount of generational quality loss.

"At the same time, one of the artists who was on our soundtrack, a guy named J.R. Swinger, got signed to a production deal with Motown. Motown picked up the *Chocolate City* title track for a compilation album and then contracted us to shoot the music video. They paid us $30,000, which back in 1994 felt like *big* money for us. As far as the film, we only had about $5,000 in cash and the rest was in-kind services. So we shot the music video and BET started running it and we got a lot of publicity and love behind us. By the time the students came back to school after the summer, they had seen the music video, heard the hype, and were seeing commercials about it on local TV. We thought we'd release *Chocolate City* in local theaters and charge students to see it. We showed a video projection of the VHS copy, which gives you an idea of the quality. We also had a whole *Chocolate City* week of activities, selling t-shirts and hats and as I'm an Alpha, we got all the Greeks to step in.

"Needless to say, the movie wound up making a lot of money in the theaters. Suddenly I'm in my fourth year of a five-year program with all this cash in a bag. I had never seen that before and it seemed like the biggest scam. It was like, Wow, you mean you'll all actually pay me to do something I like? *Chocolate City* wasn't ever about the money. It was about wanting to make a film and I've got to thank God because there were so many instances when I didn't know how things were going to happen. A lot of things, like cameras, came at the last minute but, lo and behold, we were somehow able to roll film."

Many aspiring filmmakers buy into the Hollywood myths, such as needing a film degree from a prestigious school to be taken seriously. Rob doesn't look at his lack of training in film as a disadvantage. In fact, he believes it was an asset for completing his first feature.

"Students at the film school at Florida State did shorts but never feature films. They were taught you have to have XYZ to make a film. For us it was like being poor. You don't really know you're poor so you just go and have fun. If you're born with more, you may feel like in order to have fun you have to have certain items. Well, we didn't know anything about filmmaking, so ignorance in that instance was bliss because it made the tasks not seem insurmountable. It was like, Hey, if I get a camera and some money then I can shoot a feature, right? That was our state of mind when we shot *Chocolate City*. If you're not in a position to go to film school, that doesn't mean that you can't be a great filmmaker. That shouldn't be something that holds you back.

"We also recognized that Hollywood didn't release many Black films and thought if you get a Black film made then Hollywood should come running. We contacted all the Hollywood studios and invited them to our premiere in Tallahassee, Florida, starring no one they'd ever heard of and needless to say no one came! But with the money that we made from *Chocolate City* we went on the road and took it to other cities. With the help of the Black Filmmakers Foundation, which later spawned the Acapulco and then the American Black Film Festival, we also got screenings in New York and L.A. Another company called MOBE (Marketing Opportunities for Blacks in Entertainment) brought us to Chicago. Between those screenings we wound up with a home video distribution deal with Cinequanon Pictures International. We were their first domestic release and became their highest seller. We made very little money in the end but got good exposure."

## Rainforest Films

Rob credits his partner William Packer for aiding in the creation and growth of Rainforest Films.

"Will and I have been friends since we were freshman at Florida A&M and he was one of the stars in *Chocolate City*. After the film was shot his role increased and he took over the whole marketing and promotional aspect of the film. Around that time we formed Rainforest Films (originally Rainforest Productions). The great thing is that we were two like-minded individuals. We both had a goal. My goal was to make films and his goal was to run a business, so we merged the two. We formulated a plan and took the projects on the road. Once we graduated, we decided to do Rainforest fulltime and moved to Atlanta. We encouraged each other and together have been able to blaze this independent trail, which led to films like *Trois, Pandora's Box, Motive,* and so on."

The mantra they adopted for their company was "Makin' Moves Y'all."

"When you're 'making moves' you're in constant motion," Rob explains. "You're not stagnant or staying still, so in theory you're always moving toward something. I grew up in Philly and we used to always say I'm about to make this move, meaning I'm about to make something happen, like a chess move toward your ultimate goal."

71

## Trois

At the age of twenty-four, the Rainforest partners set out to make their second feature. *Trois* is a story about a married couple who become involved in a three-way romance, which turns fatal when they find out that the third party is a lunatic. The film was financed solely by fifty non-industry investors. Affectionately called the "Furious 50," these investors were made up of middle income African Americans.

In its first weekend of theatrical release on twenty-two screens, *Trois* earned the highest per screen average of any film in the country. It went on to generate upwards of $1.3 million at the box office in just over ninety cities. Rob describes *Trois* as a film born out of necessity.

"After the *Chocolate City* experience we learned a lot," says Rob. "We made some contacts out in L.A. We did a video deal. We learned about star presence, and screenplay structure and development. At the time, bass music was the hottest thing in the country. So we wrote a bass music film and shopped it and shopped it and shopped it and actually got it in a development situation at Orion Pictures. But a merger happened, Orion dissolved, and our deal went away. We had been doing some smaller video work in Atlanta to keep the lights on and temping at a whole bunch of places. But we said, 'You know, we're filmmakers. If we're going to make a film, now's the time. Let's live and die by it or let's quit and get corporate jobs with benefits.' So we came up with a creative concept that we thought was marketable and interesting about a guy who wants to have a ménage à trois with his wife and the dynamics behind that. It was actually my partner Will's idea, which he got from being in a barbershop and listening to what people were talking about.

"Our plan was to shoot the movie digitally for about $30,000, blow it up to film, and then see if we could get a distribution deal. As we began to raise money, the money began to snowball into more money as we attached different elements. We'd get an actor and they'd say, 'Hey, if you raised $10,000 more you could shoot 16-mm. If you raise $5,000 more you could shoot 35-mm,' and the whole project got bigger and bigger. This task that started out as a $30,000 digital movie became a $200,000 35-mm movie with recognizable faces. But after making the film we took it to Hollywood and everybody passed on it.

"We were out of money and owed people so we ended up taking this film to the Acapulco Black Film Festival, and through them we got a lot of recognition and some more investors. We also decided to release the films ourselves. We had already been developing distribution relationships and marketing strategies if we're given that opportunity again, as we had previous experience with *Chocolate City*. So this time we released *Trois* on our own, and it was the road to success for us. It gave us the recognition we needed and from that we developed relationships with Sony and Columbia Tri-Star."

Rainforest Films went on to produce other memorable features, including *Pandora's Box* and *Lockdown*. With each new project, the budgets and star quality have progressively risen. Their sexy suspense feature *Motive* attracted Vivica A. Fox and Shemar Moore to the leads. The company has also crossed into the commercial world with clients the like of Coca-Cola, Ralph Lauren Polo, and GEM.

Rob Hardy and Will Packer didn't play by the rules, but their uncharacteristic approach is what ultimately propelled them to success. Filmmakers could learn a lot from these myth-breakers and their unwavering drive to go for a touchdown without a playbook in hand.

# CHAPTER 9

# Partnering for Success

*"Partnering is all about negotiation and compromise, working with someone while working around them a bit."*

GEORGINA WILLIS, POTOROO FILMS, SYDNEY, AUSTRALIA

Many filmmakers thrive on business partnerships, while for others they can be disastrous. We certainly like to think that we can work with our friends or colleagues on a daily basis, benefiting from shared experience and resources, but it is easy to make assumptions about responsibilities without formalizing a partnership agreement in writing. Before embarking on such a collaboration you should consider the advantages and disadvantages and have total confidence that you are both focused on the same goals.

The most obvious advantage of a partnership is shared responsibility. Running a film production company is an enormous undertaking and splitting the tasks, especially those nasty administrative chores that pile up, eases pressure on time. Utilizing each other's special skills is also a plus, as one person may be better at accounting while the other excels in Web site design and marketing. Ultimately, a partnership gives you the security of having someone to consult with on decisions, commiserate with over disappointments, and celebrate with during victories.

The major disadvantages are potential disputes over decisions and an unequal share of responsibility. These problems are usually the result of not having clearly delineated roles and company goals at the outset.

## Business Partnership Facts

You have a partnership when:

▶ Your business is owned by two or more people who perform the day-to-day functions of operating the business.
▶ Any partner has the authority to operate the business, spend money, and hire personnel.
▶ All partners are personally liable for debts, losses, and taxes.
▶ All partners share profits or losses.

As stated before, a legal partnership agreement will help guide a partnership and can be referred to if disputes arise. At minimum, a partnership agreement should include:

▶ roles and responsibilities
▶ percentage share of profits and losses
▶ buy-out provision (in case a partner leaves or dies)

## Potoroo Films

One highly successful partnership is Potoroo Films in Sydney, Australia. Producer/writer Kerry Rock and director/writer Georgina Willis were childhood friends who eventually partnered in 1995 with the intention of producing innovative short films and features. In recent years, their short films have been screened at over seventy international festivals in Palm Springs, Texas, Mill Valley, Seattle, Mannheim-Heidelberg, Bilbao, Grenoble, Turin, Naples, Brisbane, St. Kilda, Antalya, and elsewhere. Their first feature film *Watermark* participated in the Director's Fortnight program at the 2003 Cannes Film Festival.

Kerry and Georgina's unique personalities helped establish their roles early on.

Georgina Willis and Kerry Rock on location with *Watermark*.
(© Potoroo Films.)

"We thought alike but we knew that the two sets of skills that we had would work quite well together," reflects Kerry. "Georgina's a very imaginative, creative person and I'm probably more ordered. We have different thought processes but often come to the same conclusion. We also have different tasks so we can clearly know who's doing what."

"Even in the writing we have distinct roles," adds Georgina. "We always write things together and then I'm the director and Kerry's the producer. I'll come up with the idea and then Kerry will review the script and she'll come with her own views and then we'll discuss it quite a bit. When we get to the final part of writing the script, I put in a lot of the visuals and Kerry does a lot of the dialogue. So we're making joint decisions but we've also got distinct roles."

As both partners were untrained in filmmaking, they decided to begin with a series of shorts.

"We did six short films," explains Kerry. "Because we weren't formally trained in film, we wanted to experiment with different styles of filmmaking. The first short we did was a mix of graphic animation and real life action. It was very experimental and out there and a way of putting our toe into filmmaking. We didn't want to do something too grand or overly ambitious but it was the right path because immediately it started getting into film festivals and we thought, Oh good, we've got something happening!"

"It was also broadcast on a television station here as well," says Georgina. "So we thought this is going to work okay. With all the shorts we challenged ourselves with a different way of doing things but the key link between them was that all the films had a strong visual language and fairly minimal dialogue. We tried to build up a language that was distinct and worked for us."

The partners began Potoroo Films with limited resources, including Steinbeck editing equipment they inherited from a friend. By working as a team, they managed to successfully produce their shorts while appreciating the benefits of having a partner.

"What's kept us happy is that we have a similar view of situations and we've always felt like we could get through any situation together," says Georgina.

"Looking at others without partners, they seem to be back a few paces from where we are, even if they started out at the same time," reflects Kerry. "And in the end you need to remember that nothing should be taken so seriously, no matter what's happening. The situation will pass and you'll get through it. You've got to build some humor into these things, which we do."

Making the shorts was a critical learning phase before the partners ventured out with their first feature. Georgina advises aspiring filmmakers to go through this process rather than prematurely tackling long format projects.

"When you start out, you're sort of playing with film at that point and after you do a few short films it gives you the confidence and skills to do a feature. Features entail a whole different set of things, such as politics, that are much different from the short films. If you allow yourself to go through the short films, you'll get to the point where you'll feel like you can do a feature and you'll develop as your films develop. You also learn to handle situations. When you first start out you can find things very overwhelming and then as you go through it, everything becomes lighter."

The partners used the shorts to build their reputation through film festivals.

"Early on in the process you make a short film and wonder who's ever going to see it," says Kerry. "But once you start getting into festivals and it's working, you realize maybe what we're doing is right. Short films help get the recognition that affirms your processes and approach are working. Festivals also help get your name known so it's opening up doors and giving you a chance to meet people and build relationships. It shows people that you're very credible as filmmakers, especially in that type of an event. You've really got to get your work shown. We're making art house films and they're internationally recognized and being shown overseas."

"I think making the short films first had an impact on the Cannes selection," adds Georgina about their first feature *Watermark*. "Talking to someone who was selecting, they said they were influenced by the history of making a lot of festivals, because we'd made festivals like Palm Springs and Mill Valley and a lot of European festivals as well. It was sort of building process."

## Watermark

After the six shorts were completed, recognized, and distributed, the Potoroo partners felt ready to embark on their first feature. *Watermark* is a visually driven drama about a man whose life is determined by his relationships with the women in it. The story weaves between the 1970s and the present. Despite its deceptively gentle beginning, it builds to something more edgy and dramatic. *Watermark* is about all the things that people don't or can't say. It is an observation, like a series of portraits, with each person searching for their own way of talking in the world. *Watermark* takes a lot of risks, both in style and topic. The film is set around Sydney's beaches and the ocean, making the most of the Australian landscape.

"Everything we're trying to do is in the world of the serious drama," explains Kerry. "We're not focused on comedies or romances. We both have a strong view that we can write fairly serious stylized dramas. At the moment it's the area that's really fascinated us and where we think we can deliver the best work."

"We have our own distinct style," says Georgina. "I really think the main reason we got into the Cannes Film Festival was by being very

A production still from *Watermark*. (© Potoroo Films.)

different from other Australian films. We made *Watermark* outside of our government system. In Australia we've got government funding for films and so usually people make their projects with these funds. With *Watermark* we got government funds to finish the film. We made the film originally on 16-mm with a crew of five people and it was really an unusual way of making a feature. And then when we got into Cannes Film Festival the government film body put in a lot of money to blow the film up from 16-mm to 35-mm so it could be shown there. *Watermark* is a very shocking film as well. It involves a woman who kills her own child, so it's a very serious topic, but it allowed us to go off and be a bit strange like we'd been with our short films."

As the partners described, *Watermark* was made for very little money, so enormous effort went into the preplanning and rehearsals.

"The film has strong visuals and minimal dialogue so we had to be quite resourceful," explains Georgina. "We had a five-to-one ratio so we were using very little film. In order to do it, we had a lot of rehearsals with the actors to make sure that nothing went wrong when we filmed it.

And we managed to get through it. We spent a bit more money than we planned on but we really managed to keep our ratio down and our schedule was fairly tight because of the budget. We were really using what we learned from our short films in terms of keeping the budget down."

"We went into it with an open mind of really how challenging it was going to be," adds Kerry. "The one thing we did wrong is have too many locations. We were going from one end of the city to the other between locations that are about a hundred kilometers, apart which did bring in some logistical issues, though it was mostly to get around filming permit fees in Sydney. There were two locations we shot at for five days that you could only get to by boat. That's a challenge in itself, just the transport issues, so we planned it out fairly carefully. Having a small crew worked well because it gave us flexibility. We knew if we had to get twenty or thirty people across to this beach in the middle of nowhere, it would be too difficult. We wanted to keep the crew small and knew we could do it. People were flexible and everyone jumped in and it worked quite well. Having a small crew also made people feel they had a real part in the film."

"To save money, especially with post sound, we had really good location sound recording, and we ended up using that rather than really changing it in post," explains Georgina. "We really planned everything ahead of time to make sure it would go quite well."

The film was cut on a flatbed to save the cost of digital transfers. Despite the low budget, *Watermark* has left a distinct impression.

"For this film that started very small, it actually did make it into the international scene, which was exactly what we were hoping for," says Kerry.

"It was one of the smallest budget films," recalls Georgina. "We joke that our film had less money than those from the Third World but it actually made it to Cannes. You don't think of Australia as a Third World country but in filmmaking terms it's quite different!"

## Branching Out

While they have yet to make a profit from their films, the partners have received funding to help defray production costs and are exploring ways to expand into commercial and other work, including partnerships outside of Australia.

"We've been talking to a range of English companies looking for someone we feel is on the right wavelength and maybe has access to money over there," explains Kerry. "I think that if you want a film to reach an international audience you've got to look out the window because Australia is wonderful and fantastic but there is a cultural focus here on things being Australian. Things that are quintessentially Australian don't necessarily show well overseas. So you've got to have that external view from the beginning and think about what the rest of the world is doing. Even the smaller companies have to keep that eye outside. Australia only has about 20 million people, so when you compare that to the rest of the rest of the English speaking world, we're a blink."

Kerry and Georgina have multiple projects in different phases of development and production, which Georgina believes is critical.

"Often filmmakers will go from one project to another without a whole group of projects and that can be really difficult because something can go wrong at the last minute. So having lots of different projects happen at once has been quite effective for us."

"Another thing that can happen is that even though you think you have the most original story in the world, someone else can make something similar," adds Kerry. "Or something can happen that makes your script inappropriate for the world at this moment. We had that happen with one script where we realized it was not the time for it politically or socially. Maybe it's something we can bring out three years in the future. I think it's important to not just be committed to one project in case it doesn't go through."

With a serious commitment to their craft, a willingness to take the long road versus shortcuts, shared responsibility, and a united focus on their goals, Kerry and Georgina will certainly continue on their successful journey together.

"You have someone you can push with," concludes Kerry of the partnership. "Filmmaking is very, very challenging, both intellectually and physically. It helps to have someone you can really rely on to talk things out and help cope with the struggles that you're having."

# Finding Your Niche

*"In some shape or form you've got to make what you're doing stand out. Otherwise, people get lost and wonder, 'Who are you?'"*

LESLIE KUSSMAN, AQUARIUS FILMS, MEDFIELD, MA

S uccessful businesses are often those that have defined a "niche" and a clear picture of their customer base. Likewise, film production companies can benefit from developing a niche marketing strategy to help their unique creative offerings stand out. The niche, whether making environmentally conscious documentaries, experimental short films, snappy commercials, or horror features, becomes a useful tool for marketing your projects, securing specific clients, and enhancing your reputation as a "leader" in that area.

Do you have a niche? Ask yourself the following questions and you may be surprised to discover a very solid one.

1. What do my intended audiences have in common?
2. What differentiates my talents from others?
3. What is distinct about my company services or skills?

Sow how do you begin to answer these questions? I'll use myself as an example. Since I had many years of experience writing/producing educational healthcare media, I chose that as my main niche when I formed Amphion Productions. Given this, I would answer the above questions this way:

1. My intended audiences want to provide hospital staff with educationally sound, interactive training tools that offer continuing education credit.
2. My expertise in producing healthcare media for nationally recognized and respected organizations sets me apart from more generalized production companies.
3. Amphion Productions has produced over a hundred award-winning educational projects specifically targeted to the healthcare field.

Answering these questions will help you discover whether your company is distinct or too generic.

## Aquarius Productions

When Leslie Kussman began Aquarius Productions in Medfield, Massachusetts, over fifteen years ago, her niche came from a very personal and heartfelt goal to provide resources on life's challenges of disability, health, and bereavement. This effort has resulted in numerous international film awards including Emmys and Academy Award Nominations.

"I remember very clearly when I started my company because it was the anniversary of my mother's death," Leslie recalls. "I was nine months pregnant with my second daughter when my mom died. My background wasn't in filmmaking, but after she died I was so convinced that I had to do a film for everyone in the hospital where she worked as a social worker. I wanted everyone to have a strong image of how she influenced families and children. So I did this film called *What Do I Tell My Children?* which is about the grieving process that kids go through when they lose a loved one, and I thought the hospital would be able to give it to as many people as needed it. Well, I was very lucky and guided, and I asked Joanne Woodward to narrate it, never thinking she'd actually do it. But she agreed to do it. I've lost count but the film's won over ten awards."

*What Do I Tell My Children?* is a thirty-minute documentary that includes group discussions with parents and children who are coping with loss and interviews with leading grief counselors who offer advice on how to help a child cope with the death of a loved one. After the film was made, Leslie had no idea that what started as a small project intended for a hospital would become the nation's foremost video on coping with children and grief.

"At first I thought only people in the hospital and maybe the city would want it. Well, it ended up that people all over the country and internationally wanted it, and it's been our all-time classic bestseller. At the time I was working to raise money for Oxfam during the crisis in Ethiopia and was doing this as a side thing out of my home. I kept getting all of these phone calls or orders in the mail for copies of the film and realized eventually that I really needed to look again at what I was doing and make this film available to people around the country and really start trying to make a business to do that. That's how Aquarius got started. My sign is Aquarius and when I thought about what I was going to name the company, friends and family said, 'You should name it Aquarius because it's in memory of your mom and you have that connection,' so I did. I had a marketing rather than production background so that film was a real labor of love, and there's no way I'd have the patience now to do it the way I did. But after it came out friends started asking me to help them get their films out, and the company started growing. At first it was two, three, five, six films, and now it's five hundred plus later."

Leslie's passion to provide inspiring and important resources on health issues also comes from a very personal perspective. She has been living with multiple sclerosis for over twenty years.

"Aquarius is really about helping people to help themselves. It's about helping people not feel alone about what they're going through. I know through my personal experiences of dealing with the loss of my mom and living with a chronic illness for twenty years that you learn a heck of a lot about loss and gain, and about how to go on when you're dealing with all kinds of continuous life challenges. I walk with crutches and life isn't always easy. I have to figure a lot of different ways to make things happen, but I've got this determination that keeps me going."

Aquarius Productions' video programs offer comfort, understanding, and clarity about some of life's most challenging issues, such as coping with the loss of a loved one, acknowledging that a family member has a mental illness, struggling with the challenges of having a disability, recognizing that a spouse has a drug or alcohol problem, and deciding what is best for an aging parent who is sick. Their videos have influenced countless people, providing them with solace and inspiring them to find the courage to make necessary changes to heal.

Aquarius Productions acquires films on an exclusive basis for distribution but continues to produce its own unique projects. Leslie takes a first-hand role in these productions.

## Freedom Chasers

"I did a film last spring called *Freedom Chasers*," says Leslie. "I love the film. It's about the importance of independence for teens who have a physical or cognitive disability. I ski in a disabled skiing program and got to know all the kids in the program, and that's what inspired me to do the piece. You see people who are dealing with all of these challenges, but the challenges are not part of their life when they're out skiing. I wanted to bring that message out there, that other people who are dealing with issues can also have fun."

*Freedom Chasers* highlights the experiences of five young people and their determination to create balance, normalcy, and harmony in their lives. The young people acknowledge and accept what is different, but move far beyond their physical limitations. The viewer has the opportunity to see the passion and love for sports and outdoor activities that they feel, which is a motivating force to help them achieve their goals and dreams.

In order to get funding for projects like *Freedom Chasers*, Leslie created a separate nonprofit company called Solstice Films so the productions could be eligible for grants and sponsorship. As a distributor, Leslie also has a definitive view of the types of film projects she wants to represent.

"I'm looking for a film that I can really connect with and that really touches my heart in some way. That's very important. But also it's important to be able to connect with the producer so that their goals and my goals mesh. I think filmmakers need to ask themselves why they're doing a particular story and meditate on that to be clear. Are you doing it just to make money or get recognition or because you're trying to help other people? What's your calling? What's your relationship with the people in your story? Passion and determination is also important. I've seen people where nothing's going to get in their way of making a film happen, and that might be a corporate producer who does this at night or on the side. It might be an individual who's doing totally other things to make money but does the film on the side because they're so committed to the reason that they're doing it. It might be an issue on AIDS or a child with a learning disability or MS, you name it, but they're really drawn to it. If you're clear about why you're telling a story, it'll make what you're going for that much easier."

Leslie has seen too many filmmakers with unrealistic hopes of what they might attain from a distribution deal and cautions them to be focused at the front end of a project.

"I get so many filmmakers who call me that have maxed out their credit cards, and their friends' and spouses' credit cards, and they're trying to figure out how they can recoup it all through distribution. I think if they have a clear vision from the beginning of where they're going, what they want to spend, what's realistic and what they might reap in money from distribution, they'd be much more grounded in the process."

## Distribution

As a distributor, Aquarius Productions is primarily interested in topics of aging and gerontology, disabilities, children and teen health, alternative medicine, bereavement, caregiver concerns, women's health, nursing concerns, humor and healing, mental health, and relaxation. Leslie also looks for high-quality production and programs that are fifteen to thirty minutes in length for use in the educational and healthcare markets.

What does the producer get out of the arrangement? Aquarius takes an aggressive yet personalized marketing approach that includes packaging the video with a jacket cover, direct mail catalogs, brochures and flyers (this strategy represents 75 to 80 percent of their business), reviews in periodicals, and promotion through conferences. The company also uses telemarketing and film festival exposure to generate interest in their products.

Aquarius typically offers a three to five year contract for non-theatrical, broadcast, and home markets and assumes all marketing and promotional costs. Competitive royalties are paid on gross receipts and also include customer feedback and sales information.

As a leading provider of outstanding, award-winning videos that influence the lives of individuals facing difficult challenges, Aquarius Productions is clearly focused, with a very specific niche.

"I think it's really important to have a focus so you're not jumping all over the place," Leslie concludes. "You pick a specific niche and stay with that, or your niche is driven by the powerful stories that are told through your documentaries. Trust yourself, listen to your heart, and go forward. Have clarity on what your vision is and don't let anything get in the way."

# CHAPTER 11

# Surviving the Slow Times

*"I've often had to think outside the box to survive, however crazy that might be."*

JERRY VASILATOS, NITESTAR PRODUCTIONS, LOS ANGELES

I first met Jerry Vasilatos in Chicago in 1991 when I hired him on a friend's recommendation to sketch storyboards for a project. Since then we have become great pals, and I can best describe him as a gentle Greek teddy bear. On our first meeting, when he came limping into my office with a cane, I assumed he had recently been in an accident. The story about Jerry's leg, or lack thereof, turned out to be a fascinating tale of the complex challenges filmmakers are willing to endure in pursuit of their dreams.

## Solstice

"I wouldn't recommend that people go about funding their films this way, but the first project that I made, a Christmas movie called *Solstice* that was on Lifetime Television, was funded with the money I received from a personal injury settlement I sustained back in 1986 when I was twenty-one years old," recalls Jerry. "I was in a train accident while going to summer classes at Columbia College in Chicago and lost my leg as a result. I went back to school after the accident, but there was litigation and in 1992 the

Jerry Vasilatos on location with *Solstice*. (© 2004 Nitestar Productions, all rights reserved.)

case finally settled. By then I had already finished film school and decided I wanted a career directing movies, but I knew that no one was going to give me the money to direct my own film fresh out of college.

"So I took the risk and decided to use the money that I received from my injury, which was supposed to sustain me for years, and put it into financing a film. I had written *Solstice* as a short script that was really more of an exercise when I was going through a bad Christmas, but I had no intention of filming it at the time. When 1992 rolled around and my lawsuit settled and I was looking for a project to direct, I pulled the script out and thought it would be a very good first project because I believed it was something that people could connect with. I knew it wasn't very marketable but since my goal was to make a movie to establish myself as a director rather than make money, I wanted a good narrative story that would reach out to people. I took the money from my settlement and went into production in 1992 and finished it a year later. Again, I don't recommend that anybody go and lose a limb to finance a movie."

## The Move West

Jerry created Nitestar Productions as a banner under which to operate during the production of *Solstice*. He later incorporated and moved the company from Chicago to Los Angeles in the hope of finding more opportunities, as even with a nationally broadcast film under his belt his career had stagnated.

"I moved out to Los Angeles because even after *Solstice* was broadcast on Lifetime Television I couldn't get my directing career off the ground in Chicago," explains Jerry. "Everyone was very supportive but it wasn't the market to try to work in as a director unless I wanted to go into commercials. I wasn't going to be a feature film-maker in Chicago without money to produce another film or without connections to agents in Los Angeles. I had gone back to delivering pizzas and working at Children's Memorial Hospital in the audio-visual department. When *Solstice* was first broadcast I was also working part-time at a liquor store, which was obviously not a career highlight."

Jerry arrived in Los Angeles with a lot of hope in his heart but few resources at his disposal. Having several years of editing experience to his credit, he began freelancing as an editor to supplement his income.

"I was freelancing around town when one Christmas my father came out to visit and spent time with me while I was editing at a production house. He was interested in the equipment and asked what it would cost to get it set up. I told him it was rather expensive, but he felt it would be a good investment for my company because I could always rent it out on top of editing projects for myself. So we got a business loan and acquired an Avid editing system for Nitestar Productions. I rented an office and most of my work since that time has been editorial. It's a great tool to have when I'm producing and directing my own projects as I don't have to worry about finding an edit house and trying to negotiate a deal. On the flip side, it's an asset I have to pay off. I have to keep work coming in so that Nitestar can continue to exist while trying to get other projects off the ground as a director or producer."

## Creative Financing

When you enter the Nitestar office, the first thing you notice are shelves filled with sci-fi and adventure collectables.

"Some people collect art or baseball cards," explains Jerry. "I collect movie art because it relates to what I'm interested in. I have replicas of every treasure from the *Indiana Jones* movies and even commissioned a life-size replica of the Ark of the Covenant. It's supposed to arrive

Jerry Vasilatos (right) used his costuming skills when times were slow. (© 2004 Nitestar Productions, all rights reserved.)

in a crate, and my wife said, 'Oh good, we can put it in storage just like in the movie.' My thinking is that when we have parties, I can open it up and turn it into a beer cooler with smoked ice. On a practical level, all of the one-of-a-kind or limited movie prop replicas I've invested in might pay off in the future, in the same way art is an investment."

Jerry's interests in sci-fi and adventure have proven useful in unexpected ways.

"After editing a project starring Richard Hatch, the principle cast member of one of my favorite shows, the seventies TV series *Battlestar Gallactica*, we became friends and I ended up producing and directing a documentary retrospective for Battlestar's twenty-fifth anniversary convention. I couldn't have done it if I didn't have the editing equipment. I went out with my camera, shot all the interviews, and then cut it. My company has the potential to be a one-stop shop as far as getting projects done. I can produce and edit, and I always team up with other talented people like screenwriters, cinematographers, and other producers. So we have the means and equipment to get some interesting things done."

Jerry's sci-fi interest has been an oddball savior during slow times. When Nitestar's editing suite was idle, Jerry tapped into his collectables hobby in a unique and entrepreneurial way to keep cash flowing through the door.

"Getting through the slow times is really challenging, and you have to think outside the box and be as creative as you can. I've done some truly crazy things on the side. One example is that I collect movie costumes and props, and I found a little niche of costume collectors on the Web. I'm a big Batman fan so I knew that there were a lot of collectors who put together Hollywood-style Batman costumes, but nobody was doing the leather gloves. I discovered this because I wanted leather gloves for my own costume and when I couldn't find them, I knew that there would be people out there who needed them as well. I tracked down a glove maker and designed these authentic movie-style leather gloves with the gauntlets and fins. I ended up supporting myself for a couple months doing this little side business that was related to my background in arts and design. I sold thirty or forty pairs to a very small online market. They were inexpensive to make, but I could sell them for a fair amount. The whole process of planning, the production of the gloves, and marketing the product was very similar to filmmaking. The experiences I had as a filmmaker certainly came into play."

Jerry has an equal passion for politics from a left-wing perspective. He and his wife Lisa have been longtime activists and were unhappy with the right-wing playing decks of cards appearing on the news and Internet, especially one mocking anti-Iraqi war celebrities called *The Deck of Weasels.*

"We were offended by that," says Jerry. "We were watching the news and really wished someone did a deck of cards identifying all the chickenhawks in Congress, the Senate, and politics, and my wife and I looked at each other and said, 'If we don't do this, someone else is going to.' So in a weekend we put up a Web site for the *Deck of Republican Chickenhawks* to identify all the Republican politicians and pundits who had rallied for war but who dodged service themselves. We started getting pre-orders while we were still looking for a manufacturer to create the decks. We ended up ordering five thousand decks and soon were down to less than five hundred. We've been selling these online and at Tower Records as well as small independent bookstores. This is what has helped to support us while looking for editing work and other projects that we want to do. It was another example of saying we can do this without any plan or experience. We just jumped in, which is sometimes what you have to do. We're not a playing card business, but we figured out where to get the cards made and how to market them and through those means we were able to get some attention, such as being mentioned in *Time Magazine.* But sometimes it makes me nuts to know I'm a good editor and director yet we've had to support ourselves selling novelty playing cards and costume leather gloves!"

Prior to the 2004 presidential elections, Jerry and Lisa introduced a second deck of cards, known as *Deck of Bush: 54 Reasons Not to Re-Elect the Unelected Fraud,* which enjoyed equal success.

While these highly unusual endeavors have helped carry Nitestar Productions through the rough times, Jerry has continued on his path as a director and producer. He has been involved in multiple projects, from serious documentaries to film spoofs.

## Nitestar Projects

"I'm readying to release *Solstice* on DVD under a new title *The Night Before Christmas* because it makes it more marketable," says Jerry. "I also did a feature-length straight-to-video spoof called *The Blair Witch Rejects*, which was a slapstick parody of *The Blair Witch Project*. It was about a group of filmmakers who decide to ride the coattails of the original project by venturing out to do their own film, but they run into a bunch of other filmmakers in the forest who are doing the same thing. It's a madcap comedy spoof and something we did in a weekend. We used our own cameras and I edited the project in a couple of weeks, made the box art, and got it into Musicland stores and on Amazon.com. It's something I did to keep myself active as a director and also have fun doing.

"I also co-produced a documentary with a friend, Kevin Leadingham, called *A Refugee and Me*. It's gone on to win a number of film festival awards. It's a documentary about Kevin's friendship with a Burmese monk named Tway in Thailand. It documented Tway's experience of trying to get an identification card so he could legally have the right to work and support his family that lived on the border between Burma and Thailand. It's very touching.

"I have many other things I'm trying to get off the ground while building relationships and networking, because I really want to direct another feature film. But unless I can figure out a way to come up with the money myself, I've got to find someone who recognizes the value of what we have to offer, and that's where the networking comes in."

## How They Survive

Jerry's story shows you how much ingenuity and range is necessary in order to pursue your dream—and make a living. Here's how some of the production companies in this book generate revenue:

| | |
|---|---|
| Chip Taylor Communications | Educational distribution |
| Eshel Productions | Shuli Eshel supports Eshel with the work of her full- |

|  |  |
|---|---|
|  | service studio, Cavalcade Communications Group |
| Rainforest Films | A full service film and video production company, one that creates corporate projects, music videos, and other films for both the public and the private sector |
| Six Foot High Films | Producing and directing commercial projects |
| MotionMasters | Producing and editing corporate, commercial, and educational projects |
| Aquarius Productions | Producing and distributing health-related documentaries |
| Nightfall Pictures | Directing and producing low-budget horror films |
| Nitestar Productions | Editing documentaries and features, creating superhero gloves, playing cards, and other entrepreneurial items. |

As already mentioned, every business, no matter the size, will encounter slow times. Prepare yourself for the fact that they *will* happen. It helps to think about which skills you would most enjoy using to create revenue with your company. And, like Jerry, you may want to think of some alternative ways to keep the lights on. Perhaps you're not skilled at making customized Batman gloves, but if you are in the field of filmmaking, your creative juices will help you come up with some fresh ideas.

# PART III

# DEVELOPING YOUR OWN STYLE

# CHAPTER 12

# Rooted in Culture

*"There are dozens of people who will tell you that you can't do something. You have to be very strong in your own belief in order to tune out those messages and listen to your heart."*

RUBA NADDA, COLDWATER FILMS, TORONTO, CANADA

Ruba Nadda spent her childhood in motion, moving from Syria to different parts of Canada. Today, her storytelling is deeply grounded in her roots as an Arab and a Canadian.

"When I was young people were more racist. I was always so confused because since I was born in Canada, I didn't understand what the problem was. But the attitude was, you're not Canadian so go back to your own country. You don't belong here. When I first started making films, that began coming out. I was really adamant to show that Arabs are like everybody else. They get up every morning, eat their cereal, get on the subway, and go to work. Recently it's been even more important to break down those stereotypes that have haunted our culture for so long. My films are clips out of a person's life without a beginning, middle, or end. They also deal with human emotions. Audiences like to see themselves reflected back on screen, touching them on a deep level. I know I've managed that with my shorts, which is why I'm proud of them."

Ruba Nadda of Coldwater Films

Frequent moves can be traumatizing at a young age, as children crave stability and familiarity. Only as an adult can Ruba appreciate the benefits, which are reflected in her films.

"Whenever someone asks me where I'm from, I say I don't know," says Ruba. "It's tough because you never really fit in, and I think that's great when you become an adult because it makes you stronger and more driven, whereas people who've lived somewhere their whole lives have that safety. My sisters and I began to have a much better understanding of people and where they're coming from, so I'm not judgmental. I see the beauty in people's flaws and problems, and I think a lot of my themes in filmmaking touch upon what it means to have a home or be displaced; what it means to have an identity or be Canadian or Arab. Many of my shorts are about people with some serious flaws but it's overlooked because of the situation. I don't think I would have had this perspective if I hadn't been uprooted so many times."

Ruba has a strong disdain for the golden handcuffs of the corporate world, which compelled her into the creative realm of filmmaking.

"In university I was mortified at the prospect of graduating and getting a nine-to-five job," she admits. "As naïve as I was, I thought that I could start making films and earn a living from it. Little did I know! So I went to NYU to study for a summer and then began making films."

Ruba's early start in Canada was difficult, especially having been trained in the United States.

"The biggest problem for me was that I wasn't educated in film in Toronto and that was held against me and how I made my films was really unacceptable to a lot of people. The approach I was taught in New York is 'shut up and go make your movie. Don't worry about production value and real actors but concentrate on your story and get the film made.' That's exactly what I did. I came back and taught friends how to use sound and a boom, taught them to act, and started making films that were really well received everywhere in the world but Canada."

## Coldwater

Ruba's feature film *Coldwater* centers on a Muslim woman in her forties who still lives with her very traditional family.

"The family and culture run her life," explains Ruba. "It's not heavy-handed. They don't lock her up in her room, but subliminally there's a pressure to follow the traditional ways. One day she falls in love and decides to act on it with a Caucasian man. It's a lighthearted drama about a woman who finally takes control of her life."

After working independently on all her shorts and feature-length films, Ruba teamed up with a producer, Tracey Boulton, to make *Coldwater*, and together they formed Coldwater Productions. It was Ruba's first experience of working with a partner.

"It was hard at first because there was someone else who had an opinion, and I'm like, 'No, your opinion should be like mine!' My partner Tracey will disagree with me on creative issues, and I'll give her opinions about producing, so there's compromise with a partner. But the good stuff outweighs the bad because you have someone going through the same experience and helping make it happen. The best part is having someone to go to when things get tough."

The Coldwater partners managed to get full financing for their feature, a far different cry from Ruba's earlier experiences.

"Recently out of university I made a short film that was very ambitious," remembers Ruba. "I was working full-time and put every thing into that film. It ended up being a total disaster. I was evicted from my apartment and had to sleep on friends' couches. The worst thing is that the film didn't go anywhere. It just sat on my shelf and I was devastated.

"But then I got an idea for a five-minute short and thought, What the hell. I literally had one roll of film and five hundred dollars to my name. So I made *I Do Nothing* about a twelve-year old girl who stops men on a street corner and asks them if they think she's beautiful. That film went on to show at over 400 festivals. Originally I was going to use a woman in her mid-twenties, but thought it would be so interesting to cast my younger sister in it, which I did. That film's my favorite because it had so much promise and hope. That's the whole point of this industry. It's not so much about talent as how long you can stick it out."

## The Importance of Shorts

Like other filmmakers in this book, such as Kerry Rock and Georgina Willis of Potoroo Films in Australia or Emma Farrell from Six Foot High Films in England, Ruba sees the value of tackling a number of shorts before attempting a feature.

"I've known filmmakers who have made one short, polished film that's been critically acclaimed in festivals, and they suddenly want to jump into a feature," says Ruba. "I tell them it's crazy as they won't get taken seriously. I made twelve short films and two indie features before I was taken seriously, and in retrospect I'm glad that happened because I've made so many mistakes along the way. Now I'm prepared for a feature, as I won't make the same mistakes. It's really hard to make the jump from a five-minute film to a full-length ninety-minute film. In this industry you don't usually get more than one chance, so if you make some bad mistakes you're screwed. I've seen plenty of filmmakers who made features that bombed after a successful short. Or they got their big break and were so scared of making mistakes that they ended up making really safe movies. I'm not afraid to make mistakes. To this day I don't know the right lingo on the set, but I don't care if I say something wrong. Mistakes happen but you move on.

"At least with all my shorts and independent features I didn't waste anybody's money but my own. That ended up being a real selling point to the financiers of *Coldwater*. They saw I'd paid my dues. The whole process takes a long time, and that's important for filmmakers to know. Your film won't happen in a month or even a year. It took two years to finance *Coldwater* and that's considered fast."

Paying dues meant years of temping while juggling many projects and ideas.

"I'm the queen of being an executive assistant," laughs Ruba. "I've had to temp a lot, though in the past two or three years not as much. Meanwhile, I think it's smart to have multiple projects going on. Right now I have six in development at various stages so I don't have to wait every three years to make a film."

Part of *Coldwater's* funding success came from exposure through festivals in European markets, reiterating the importance of festival exposure.

"If I hadn't had the European festival exposure, I wouldn't be here right now," claims Ruba. "Part of our financing came from Europe and from selling rights to sales agents and distributors there. Those companies knew who I was as they'd seen my films in, and I was often touted as a festival's discovery or some European country's discovery and the region was just a lot more open to my films and happier to nurture me along with this particular project. I'd had so many rejections in Canada but didn't give up. I just kept sending my films around the world to see where they would be accepted and that's what took me to the next level."

## Unsettled

In addition to her shorts, Ruba wrote and directed a feature called *Unsettled* before embarking on *Coldwater*. Unlike *Coldwater*, she had no outside financing for this project, yet for all of its challenges it is very close to her heart. *Unsettled* is a low-budget 16-mm film that follows the life of Randy, a drug dealer, over the course of four pit stops that show how his life is becoming ensnared by intimacy and responsibility.

*Unsettled* was great because I did it on my own, so I was making all the decisions without input from financers and so forth. I was also working with the same cast and crew since I first started making films, so it was really enjoyable. But at the end of the day it broke my heart. I had to turn down many film festivals because at the time festivals only showed prints. Because I shot *Unsettled* on Super 16 I didn't have a print and certainly couldn't afford to blow it up to 35-mm. *Coldwater* is much more professional with a bigger budget, and we have a theatrical distributor, so there's a print at the end of the day."

Fortunately, Ruba's family has provided a strong support system through her tumultuous but prospering career.

"They're so happy and have been so supportive. There's a part of me that feels so bad because I know if I don't make it, they'll be devastated, as now their hearts are tied to my goals and dreams. That's a scary thing. We always have these dreams and there's never a guarantee, but now my dream is really finally coming through."

Learning not to take rejection too personally has also helped Ruba weather the hard times.

"I take rejection personally like any other artist, but the next day I'm back at it again. You have to be like that because no one is going to believe in your project and you more than yourself. If you don't believe in what you're doing, then why should anyone else? My motto is you never know what's going to happen, so you might as well try. You have to think positively for positive things to happen. People will try to bring you down but if you have a dream that you want to attain, then create a path and follow it."

## Film Festival Exposure

As Ruba and other filmmakers in this book reiterate, film festivals are probably the most valuable form of exposure for short films, since there are few venues that screen shorts for the general public. Short films are never created with the idea of making money, but as "calling cards" that showcase a filmmaker's talent and creativity.

However, film festival submission prices can be steep, not to mention the cost of attending. It is important to strategize the best festival opportunities for your particular project so the process is not too daunting.

While the application process differs between festivals, you will typically be asked to submit the following for consideration:

- ▶ An application form (usually available as a download on most festival Web sites)
- ▶ A film, Beta, or digital video copy of your project
- ▶ Crew and talent credits
- ▶ A press kit
- ▶ Production stills (if available)
- ▶ Application fee

If your film is accepted into a festival, it is worth attending for numerous reasons. In addition to the possibility of receiving an award, it is a great networking opportunity and a chance for you to see how audiences react to viewing your film on the big screen. Especially if your film is a short, it may be the one time you get that live theatrical excitement. For more about film festivals, see the Film Festival section in chapter 18, Marketing Strategies.

# CHAPTER 13

# The Making of a PBS Documentary

*"You have to believe very strongly in the quality of your work in order to tune out negative messages and listen to your heart."*

DIANA SOLE, MOTIONMASTERS, CHARLESTON, WV

Diana Sole, President of MotionMasters.

**M**otionMasters in Charleston, West Virginia, is not your typical film and video production company, internally or externally. Built on a large plot of land, the building is more reminiscent of a rambling, country lodge than a corporate center.

"We told the architect the very first thing we want you to do is throw out any preconceived notions you have of corporate environments," says president Diana Sole. "We wanted something that was much more homelike in structure. It needed to be very high-tech internally, with certain parameters, but we wanted an atmosphere that lent itself to a creative environment. For example, all of the windows in this building have screens, so several months of the year we open the windows and let the breezes blow in. It's wonderful and so unusual to have fresh air in a modern building these days. We built almost one thousand feet of porches on the building including one in the back that runs the full length of the second floor and overlooks the treetops the way the land is graded here. We can walk out on this wonderful wooded porch for creative sessions with our clients, and they love it. And we literally have these sessions sitting on rocking chairs. We also built a full kitchen, as many of us like to cook. If we have a client who's been camped in the editing room all day, we'll plan to cook a meal in the kitchen and everybody comes and sits down at the table like a big Thanksgiving dinner. We wanted the kind of environment where people felt at home and comfortable, where clients knew that they were friends, not just a meal ticket."

Like the building, Diana Sole is no ordinary woman. I've always considered Diana an icon of sorts. When I worked for her company as a producer/writer back in 1991, I was awed by her amazing skills of persuasion. With graceful, subtle finesse, she exuded a hypnotic power that lured almost any prospective client she wanted through the door. I believe it is this power of persuasion, combined that a solid conviction toward her craft, that is responsible for MotionMasters' success with their nationally broadcast documentaries.

## A Principled Man

MotionMasters' first PBS long-format documentary was *A Principled Man: Reverend Leon Sullivan*. This powerful biography documents the life of Reverend Leon H. Sullivan, founder of the African-American Summit, long-time proponent of self-help for people of all races, and the first African American on the board of directors at General Motors. In 1977, Reverend Sullivan formulated what became known as his "legacy," the Sullivan Principles, a set of ethical directives calling for equitable treatment for South African workers. These guidelines were instrumental in the abolishment of apartheid.

The idea for the documentary happened by circumstance, while MotionMasters was producing a thirty-minute program about successful West Virginians, past and present, called *The West Virginians.*

"In doing the research for that project we came across the name of Reverend Leon Sullivan and learned a little bit about what he had done with his career," explains Diana. "He was one of the nine current-day individuals who we profiled, and the more we learned about him, the more intrigued we became. We were enamored with his story and felt that he needed to be the subject of his own documentary. I was quite surprised to find he had not been the subject of a documentary at that point, nor had he published a biography of his life. So the thought came to me that somebody ought to do this. And the more I thought about it, the more I realized *we* could do this. So we started down the track of trying to pull together the resources, finances, and contacts to put together the documentary. The first thing I did was attend a conference with seminars on producing documentaries and raising funds. I also bought a pile of books and said, Okay I'm ready to roll up my sleeves and do this."

The first challenge was to convince Reverend Sullivan that his story needed to be told.

"He was a very humble man and when I approached him about the idea he was very reticent to do it," Diana recalls. "He said, 'Diana, I'm seventy-three-years old and I haven't tooted my own horn. Why should I start now?' So I just worked at convincing him that his story was a powerful, inspirational one that I believed people needed to hear. It took me six to nine months of phone calls back and forth to convince him that not only should he tell his story, but he should allow us to be the ones to tell it. Ultimately he agreed and I started to look for a fiscal sponsor with which to work."

Diana Sole on location with Reverend Leon Sullivan.

## Fiscal Sponsorship

Many documentary makers gain fiscal sponsorship, meaning teaming up with a nonprofit organization for the production, to leverage donations that are tax deductible.

"Corporate donors want to be able to give to something for which they get a tax credit," Diana explains. "In this case I approached a few nonprofit entities for their support in the project as a sponsor and really couldn't get anybody to understand what it was I was trying to do. West Virginia is not a hotbed of film and video production, so the whole concept of a fiscal sponsorship was foreign. I was turned down several times and then I went to Marshall University, which is the school from which I graduated, and talked to them about it. Coincidentally, Reverend Sullivan was coming in to speak during Black History Month, and the senior vice president and assistant to the president went to hear him speak. I told them we were taping the presentation because we wanted to get to the point where we could do a documentary about Reverend Sullivan's life. The senior vice president was so inspired by the reverend's message that day that after the event he came up to say, 'What can we do to help you make this happen?' I said, 'Well, you can step in as the fiscal sponsor!' He took my proposal to the president of Marshall University and within a couple of days I had an answer, and the answer was, 'Yes, we'd be delighted to do this.' So then I had the financial structure with which to go out and begin to raise money."

## Fundraising

Most of the donations came from corporations and foundations, many from supporters of Reverend Sullivan's work in social activism. But raising these funds was hardly an overnight process.

"It involved several years of raising money while doing production in tandem," says Diana. "I'd be out raising money at the same time we were shooting and just trying to chase the project that way. At the time we already had ten, twelve years in business producing corporate productions so a lot of the donors were people with whom we had worked for years who were familiar with our work and our standards, so they had a comfort level giving to the production. They knew that a quality product was going to be the end result. I know sometimes people get funny about corporate versus documentary work and that you should produce either one or the other. I think doing both enhances both. And there is no doubt the fact that we did that documentary has helped us win more corporate work also."

Perseverance was critical to raising enough funds to cover a budget that included several trips to Africa.

"There were so many times in the process during that I threw my hands up in the air and didn't know what to do because I'd hit a wall," admits Diana. "I'd contacted every person I knew to contact. I'd asked for every nickel and dime that I could find and I didn't have enough to finish the production. But something else would happen which would allow us to get to the next stage. It would have been very easy to give up and in fact people outside *and* inside the company said give it up. But I didn't because I believed in the story and I just kept finding ways to make it happen.

"A lot of the donors were people who initially turned us down. We went back to them, usually in their next funding cycle, and said here we are again. And we're here because we're convinced that this is a story you want to be a part of and we'd like for you to reconsider. One entity that we went to made the remark, 'Why should I give money to a no-name entity in West Virginia?' Well, we went to her boss and got the money anyhow. So the most important message I'd like to convey to people who are committed to telling a story but don't see the path yet is that you just have to be persistent, and sometimes downright stubborn."

## Working with PBS

Stubbornness won out, and the documentary was finished and ready for distribution. This presented another set of challenges, again calling for Diana's unique power of persuasion.

"West Virginia Public Broadcasting was our local sponsoring station, which you have to have for national consideration. The process for submitting the documentary to national for review was not easy. When the national PBS first reviewed it, they decided it would be a good piece for their regional feeds but didn't want to broadcast it on the PBS 'hard' schedule. I wasn't satisfied with that. I said no, I want a commitment for a national broadcast and if you're only interested in it for the regional feeds then I'm pulling it back. Well, they didn't like that. They looked at the piece again and decided they were now interested in a national feed but asked us to change some content. One of PBS's rules is that you can't have someone mentioned in the piece who is also an underwriter. In this case General Motors was an underwriter, and we had the former chairman of General Motors as an interviewee on the tape. We had to have this man. They were telling me I had to take him out because of their rule, but he was the only person who actually said outright, 'White corporate America didn't like this Black man, some preacher from West Virginia, telling them what to do.' It was a critical piece to have in the documentary, and I fought hard to keep it in.

"There were a couple of minor things they also wanted us to change and I said no, we're not going to and again, I am pulling this piece back out because what you're trying to take out is essential to the story, and I'm not going to ruin it by deleting things from the tape. So a couple weeks went by with those types of negotiations, and ultimately they took the documentary entirely as we produced it and ran it as a national broadcast."

*A Principled Man: Reverend Leon Sullivan* was also edited and packaged as an educational video with supporting print materials. Diana took care in selecting the non-broadcast distributor, looking for a company that could cross-market the project over several types of curriculum, from African-American studies to economics. She settled on the University of California in Berkley's media center.

"You need to find a distributor who you know has a proven track record of selling material in the same topical area," Diana advises. "Also, a company willing to commit resources to promote the documentary so it gets the exposure it needs."

## In the Pipes

MotionMasters' second documentary profiles the life of Senator Robert Byrd of West Virginia. A third, about the life of former U.S. Supreme Court Chief Justice John Marshall, is also nearing completion.

"I thought having one documentary under my belt would make the next one easier, but the truth is it's not!" laughs Diana. "So again, we just kept plugging and plowing ahead. You have to keep moving forward, chipping away at it piece by piece and somehow you'll get there. I think we'll continue to do documentaries on people like Sullivan and Byrd who had very humble origins but have done truly remarkable things. They've not allowed their birth or situation in life to hold them back from achieving some pretty astounding results. I'm drawn to stories of people who overcome incredible odds to do wonderful things. People who don't sit back and say, Oh, woe is me. Instead they say, *Watch me!*"

People have certainly watched MotionMasters with the same wonder over the years. Among many awards and other recognition, Diana and her business partner Dan Shreve received the 2001 Entrepreneur of the Year award from Ernst and Young, an awards program designed to recognize individuals who are paving the way for a new age of entrepreneurship.

When Diana reflects on all of the trials and tribulations she has experienced as a production company owner, she boils down her advice to a simple tenet.

"Don't worry about what you don't know. Concentrate on what you do know. Concentrate on perfecting your craft, on producing good material. It doesn't matter whether that's something for the corporate world or one of your own projects. Be proud of what it is you're doing. If you're not happy with it, then don't let it get out. Put in the extra effort to make it what it should be and could be."

# CHAPTER 14

# A Horrifying Experience

*"People wonder if I had a bad childhood but I think it's usually those who have really normal childhoods who like horror films because they're an escape from boring suburban life."*

BRAD SYKES, NIGHTFALL PICTURES, LOS ANGELES

I first met Brad Sykes through his wife Josephina, a screenwriter and production coordinator from Bucharest, Romania, a place I have visited many times myself. We equally enjoy this Eastern European country's timeless beauty and intelligent, spirited people, not to mention unique regional delicacies such as sarmale (cabbage rolls) and grilled mititei (handmade, seasoned sausages). Over such meals and a few bottles of wine, we discovered we also shared a similar interest in films, especially those of the horror/thriller genre.

Brad's favorite oldies include *Dawn of the Dead* and *Texas Chainsaw Massacre*. He describes horror as "the most cinematic genre with plenty of room to experiment with various themes." Brad has made a career as a director in this unique industry.

"I think it's hard for any horror fan to really explain why they like the genre so much," says Brad. "There are images that you can present in a horror film that you wouldn't be able to present in other genres, and that's very liberating and fun. At the same time, there are certain patterns and structures that are somewhat inescapable in the genre that

Brad Sykes on location with *Death Factory*. (Photo credit: Josephina Sykes.)

can get repetitive, so as a filmmaker you try to mix it up, like combining horror with other genres. It's also about who you're working for, who you're working with, and how willing they all are to go along for the ride and try something new."

At an early age, Brad knew he wanted to become a director of horror films and moved from Virginia to Los Angeles to pursue his dream.

"Like a lot of people, I graduated film school and moved right out here," says Brad. "I worked on different movies as a PA and director's assistant. I had made about eight video movies in Virginia, both in high school and during college. They really were amateur projects but feature length and fairly professional for that level. One day I was a PA on a movie and was talking to the producer, and I mentioned that I had directed some stuff. He asked to see one of my movies, and then he hired me to write and direct something for him, which was a pretty low-budget project. But that was how it all started for me."

## Mad Jack

Brad continued making low-budget films, primarily for distribution companies. A turning point came in 1999 with the production of *Mad Jack*.

"*Mad Jack* was my fifth movie, but the ones before that were exploitation movies based on other people's ideas or concepts. *Mad Jack* was the first one I directed based on an idea I came up with, and it was only the second movie I made that was shot on film. I put together two different financial entities to get it made. I got part of the money from Virginia and part of it here. Did that movie really move my career along? No, but personally and professionally it was a big step forward."

One of Brad's funding sources came from a friend in Virginia.

"I'd known him for at least five or six years, and he really wanted to make a movie," explains Brad. "Of course, he wanted to star in it. That's the Ed Wood part of the story. He and I had worked on some shorts together off and on. While we were doing these really small projects he was putting aside money here and there and saved up enough to make a feature. We were going to shoot it on video, but I had just done a film for Vista Street, which is a small distribution company known mainly for the *Witchcraft* series. There are twelve of them, and I directed the last one, so I don't know if that'll be the final nail in the coffin or not!

"Anyway, I had already done one movie for Vista Street and decided to take a chance to see if we could double the funding for *Mad Jack*. I spoke with Jerry Feifer, the head of the company, and said look, I've got a guy coming out here who's got $10,000 and we're going to do this movie on video with ten grand if we have to, but if you want to put up the same amount you could be a partner in this film and take care of the post. Then you would have some ownership on the film. Jerry said yes, though in exchange for putting in a certain number of sex scenes. It sounds absurd but that's how some of these guys are—the script is built around the sex. Then your challenge is to motivate them without coming off like total trash. There were two things I did to get around that. First, I didn't shoot the sex scenes as he probably thought I would. For example, I shot one as a single long take with no nudity and in a far more dramatic way than he was expecting.

Of course that made him really mad but by then it was too late to change it. I also turned some of the other scenes into thriller/murder moments. There's a little bit of sex and then somebody gets killed by the psychotic killer in the story. Secondly, I was lucky to have a very sympathetic editor who would take my side over the executive producer's, which is not something that always happens, so we cut the scenes down as much as we could. Obviously there was going to be some nudity in the film but I don't have a problem with the way it turned out. I've shown it to a lot of people and nobody has said, Oh god, there's a lot of sex and nudity in this film.

"At the same time, you've also got to keep people happy. If somebody gives you money you can't just go off and make a totally different film than they expect because you won't get a good reputation that way. It's a tough game. You have to try to see everyone's point of view. But in the case of *Mad Jack* we got away with something."

## Picking Your Battles

The control issues Brad mentioned are commonplace to filmmakers whose funding comes from outside sources such as investors or distributors, as discussed earlier in this book. Brad is happiest with the films on which he put up the biggest fights for creative control.

"I don't think I've ever made anything that I really cared about that I didn't have to fight tooth and nail to get it the way I wanted it to be. *Death Factory* isn't by any means a groundbreaking movie, but I accomplished what I set out to do with it and I was really happy with it technically. There are other films where you have the chance to try something different, like *Goth*, which we shot entirely handheld and spent a lot of time on the sound design. You pick your battles. You learn quickly that you're not going to be able to do that on every film so you try to make those decisions early on and stick to your guns on the ones that matter most. There are true assignments where I'm given a script that's not particularly good with real budget limitations. So I say okay, I'm going to deliver the best movie I can but I'm not going to shed blood and tears for this one. Some people are amazed to hear that because they expect directors to kill themselves over every film they make and I've worked with directors who will do that, but it doesn't always behoove you. Save your energy for your personal films. Not necessarily one you have to fund with your own money, though often that's what it comes down to."

Brad remembers how creative control issues sometimes had a serious impact at the worst of times.

"*Demon's Kiss* was an erotic horror film about a woman who gradually turns into a monster. We had already shot half the movie and were shooting the ending of the film at three in the morning when the executive producer decided that he didn't want the monster in it. We literally shot two different endings, which for films with these budgets and schedules is ridiculous. There just isn't time to do that. We did anyway but I already knew which ending we were going to use because I knew the person who was controlling the film financially was going to have the advantage."

Working with small budgets, Brad appreciates the collaborative process involved in completing a film.

"The more help you can get, the better, and there's always good help out there. I've seen too many projects where people tried to do it all by themselves and it didn't help the film."

## Jobs for Hire

Brad has taken his share of flack over the years from other filmmakers who question some of the projects he's undertaken. He brushes it off, knowing he's at least making money in the industry while improving his skills.

"These are often people who haven't made anything so it's kind of easy to snipe from the corners. I'm not proud of everything I've done. In fact, I kind of wish I could take my name off a few things. But you know what? I've been fairly busy since I've been out here and you never know what's going to happen with these films. Sometimes they really take off. I know a lot of guys who do the ultra-low-budget independent stuff where there's no funding and a lot of time between projects. I like to work and to make films. I've got stuff in Hollywood Video and Blockbuster and Best Buy, and people can look me up and see this guy's actually done something. I think that commands some respect from the actors and crews I work with. It also gives you a lot of experience to draw from in terms of problem-solving, and these movies are all about problem-solving. With every movie there's going to be some weird thing that comes up because everything's so compromised.

"When I did *Mad Jack* in the Mojave Desert, the last day of shooting was a twenty-four-hour day. You press people that much and they're going to get mad, so tensions were running high. I've had shoots get rained out, people get into car accidents and late to the set, and the usual problems with permits, or lack thereof. I've made sixteen movies and never had a permit, except for one scene at a college in *Death Factory*. That's definitely taking a risk. For *Mad Jack* we were shooting at a totally abandoned gas station that had been closed for god knows how long. It was a short scene but it would take a few hours to do. We had laid down dolly track when some guy comes over from across the street yelling at us, and it turned out to be the owner of the gas station. He wanted to call the police and had his cell phone out. That's when the director becomes the diplomat. Please don't call the cops, we're just doing this little student film. When in doubt, say it's a student film. His main problem was that he didn't want a bunch of trash left there, even though the place was already a total dump. We said okay, this place is going to be cleaner when we leave than when we got here. So we picked up the bottles and cans lying around to get a free gas station location. It's a very tense way of making a movie because you're not just worried about finishing on time, you're also worried about someone showing up and kicking you out."

Today Brad feels as though he has hit a ceiling in his career as a horror film director and is shifting his career goals.

"You either come out of the gate with a movie like *Cabin Fever* or *Blair Witch* or you don't. If you do one ultra-low-budget horror movie, then you're going to be given another ultra-low-budget horror film and it's definitely a cycle and you can be trapped in. I'm definitely ready to get out of that. Right now I'm working on some scripts for a few producers who saw some of my work and hopefully that will translate into something bigger. I'm not trying to get another ultra-low-budget horror film. I've paid my dues in that area, and I've already got some things that speak pretty well for me, so doing another one isn't necessarily going to change my life one way or another."

## Grounded in Reality

Brad has a very grounded attitude about the film industry and suggests other filmmakers be as realistic about the movie-making process.

"You're going to go through so many projects that will not get off the ground. And this is going to sound incredibly pessimistic, but you must be prepared to take a bath on your first film. If you're making it yourself with your own cash, just make the best movie you can. Don't worry about how much money you think you can make back. I don't think it's realistic to make any assumptions, like this project is going to net this much from this territory or whatever. There are only certain genres of movies that sell well in film markets internationally and horror is one of them. The independents that get reported are the success stories, like *Blair Witch* and *Clerks*. But that whole nineties indie explosion is really over if you think about it. I think studios and independent divisions of studios are getting a lot choosier about what they pick up."

With Brad's pragmatic perspective on the industry and his future, combined with skill and a passion for the craft, his director and screenwriting credits should appear in many more films, not just in the local video stores but on the big screen. As they say for good luck in Romania, *Noroc*!

# CHAPTER 15

# Not Short on Style

*"Other people gamble on the lottery and horses, but I like gambling on myself and on my talent. I think that's a worthwhile gamble."*

BILL PLYMPTON, PLYMPTOONS, NEW YORK CITY

I was very excited when Bill Plympton agreed to be interviewed for this book, as the foremost question in my mind was how can you possibly make a living as an independent animator, especially one so far adrift from the "commercial" world of the genre? While Bill may not be reaping the financial success of his Hollywood peers, he has discovered a far greater reward.

"It's a wonderful feeling to get up in the morning with the freedom to do the silliest ideas in the world. They could be stupid or bad or a waste of time but at least you're doing what you want to do. Conversely, you don't make a lot of money. If I were to work for Disney or Dreamworks I would have restrictions but I'd be making a lot more money and have more security. That's a question all artists have to ask themselves; what's their priority? Is it to make money, raise a family, and have a house, or do you want to be an artist who will probably suffer, at least early on? Now I make good money but initially it was very difficult to get started. I'm not being judgmental. There are a lot of great animators working for Disney and Dreamworks who I admire, and in a way

I'm a little jealous of their fame and income. At the same time, there's no producer, director, lawyer, or agent looking over my shoulder telling me to change the art because it might offend someone or hurt sales."

Bill's distinctive animations offer an oblique, off-center sense of the ridiculous in everyday life. His shorts and features have won numerous awards, including a 1988 Oscar nomination for Best Animation. But his success is only the result of very hard work and a deep passion for his craft. Born in Portland, Oregon, to a large family, Bill credits the rainy climate and an early love of the genre for nurturing his drawing skills and imagination.

"I'm one of the guys that grew up watching a lot of the *Bugs Bunny*, *Daffy Duck*, and *Road Runner* films. I love really violent, crazy, fast-paced stuff. Marx Brothers humor was a big influence as well. I especially liked Charles Addams, creator of the *Addams Family*. I consider him the godfather of a lot of this dark humor that is so popular today. He was one of the few cartoonists who made fun of people being eaten by snakes and having terrible accidents or getting boiling oil poured on their head. As a young kid I thought this was tremendously funny. So it's only natural that as an adult I still find these cartoons hilarious and like the anti-Disney aspect of them. I think there are people out there who want something a little darker and edgier."

Bill attended Portland State University, where he edited the yearbook and was a member of the film society. His first attempted animation was for the film society, making a yearbook promo that was accidentally shot upside-down, rendering it totally useless.

To avoid the Vietnam War, Bill served in the National Guard from 1967 to 1972. In 1968, he moved to New York City and began a year of study at the School of Visual Arts. As a recent graduate, he tried unsuccessfully to pay his rent by selling belts on the street.

"It was January, about twenty-five degrees outside," he recalls. "I couldn't sell a one!"

In time, Bill's illustrations began gracing the pages of the *New York Times*, *Vogue*, *House Beautiful*, the *Village Voice*, *Screw*, and *Vanity Fair*. His cartoons appeared in such magazines as *Viva*, *Penthouse*, *Rolling Stone*, *National Lampoon*, and *Glamour*. In 1975, in the *Soho Weekly News*, he began *Plympton*, a political cartoon strip, which became syndicated in over twenty papers by Universal Press. Although Bill loved illustration, ignorance was keeping him from his ultimate goal.

"I've made gazillions of mistakes. The first one was not getting into animation earlier. After I graduated from art school I should have followed my heart and my background, as from the age of three or four I wanted to be an animator. I had this impression that to be an animator you had to work at a Disney studio or at Warner Brothers and really know the whole business inside out, so I felt like I'd be wasting my time. I went right into illustration and cartooning, which is something I love to do. I wasn't totally disappointed but in the back of my mind I still had this desire to do animation.

"So after about twelve or thirteen years of being an illustrator/ cartoonist I had an opportunity to make an animated film. And it was through that opportunity that I found out about a whole world of animation that I wasn't aware of like, the film festival circuit; MTV was starting to buy animation, and there was a big market for animated shorts in Europe. I was really ignorant about the market for my animation and if I knew then what I know now, I would do animation right out of school and go to these film festivals that are there to promote animation. There are thousands of festivals now that provide a whole network for marketing and merchandizing your film."

## Boomtown

This first opportunity to make an animation came in 1983 when Valeria Vasilevski of the Android Sisters singing group asked Bill to work on a film she was producing of Jules Feiffer's song, *Boomtown*. Immediately following the completion of *Boomtown*, he began his own animated film, *Drawing Lesson #2*. Production of the live action scenes was slow, so Bill decided to start on another film, *Your Face*, in which a second-rate crooner sings about the beauties of his lover's face while his own face metamorphosizes into the most surreal shapes and contortions possible. For this short, he contacted Maureen McElheron, an old friend with whom he had performed in a country western band. Maureen agreed to score the project, and due to budgetary considerations she also sang, even though the animation required a male voice. Her voice was decelerated to sound more masculine, and combined with a fantastically contorting visage the film garnered a 1988 Oscar nomination for Best Animation, propelling Bill's career furiously forward. His work began appearing on MTV and in the increasingly popular touring animation festivals. *Your Face* became one of the most profitable short films ever made, still showing the world over. Fortunately, Bill was wise enough to retain ownership of the project.

"After finishing *Boomtown*, a Russian immigrant saw the film and said he'd be happy to finance my next film. I was really excited and thought, Gee, this guy is giving me free money to make a film. This is perfect. But as I was lying in bed that night I thought, Wait a minute. He's going to own the film and if he doesn't like something he can threaten to retract his money and I won't be able to finish it. So I called him the next day and said I've got $3,000 and I'd rather just invest in my own project. That was the smartest thing I ever did because *Your Face*, which cost about $3,000, went on to make about $30,000 and it's still making me money. I think it's a question that every filmmaker has to ask themselves. How strongly do you believe in the film and how much money do you have in the bank to finance it? The great thing about animation is that it's really evergreen. It never ages. Look at something like *Snow White and the Seven Dwarves*, which came out in '38 or '39, and now the film is making more money than it did over sixty years ago. Animation has a timeless quality that is unique, and that's why I really want to retain the copyright to my films.

"With all these new formats coming out like DVD and the Internet, and new markets opening up like China and the Far East, there's always a place for this stuff, and the bigger my name becomes, the more money I can get for my films. I think to lose the ownership of my films would be suicidal. Initially it's very expensive to finance your own films and it's rigorous, but once you get to a stage like where I am now, it's quite easy. Another good example is Don Hertzfeldt. He was nominated for an Oscar for a film called *Rejected*. He makes the crudest stick figure drawings you ever saw but the humor is so rich and unique that his films made a lot of money. He also self-finances, and although he's only made about six short films, his stuff is always in demand. So he was very smart to retain ownership and copyright of the films."

## Bill's Rules for Animated Shorts

Bill has three rules for making successful animated shorts.

"Number one is to make the film short. Around five minutes is a perfect length. Two, make it inexpensively, because if you spend a lot of money on special effects, orchestral music, or digital technology, it's going to be hard to make your money back. I recommend making it for about $1,000 to $2,000 per minute. A lot of people use Flash and you can make it for even cheaper than that. And three, I think it should be funny. If you're trying to sell a film to a TV network or compilation films for the theater or Internet, people want to see funny films, so those are much easier to sell. If you can do that and can bang out about two shorts a year, after a while you'll build up a nice library of films. Right now I have twenty to thirty short films that I keep selling over and over again. The problem, of course, is getting started. That's why I recommend that you initially work in a company to get a bankroll to help you through the first two years. If you can get through the first two years and your films are funny, I think it's pretty easy to continue the business."

After a string of highly successful short films (*One of Those Days*, *How to Kiss*, *25 Ways to Quit Smoking*, and *Plymptoons*), Bill began thinking about making a feature film, his dream since childhood.

## The Tune

Bills first full-length feature, *The Tune*, is about a songwriter who is given forty-seven minutes to write a hit or lose his job and his sweetheart. Bill personally drew and colored 30,000 cels for the project. Again, Maureen McElheron provided the score. As with his shorts, Bill financed the film himself, although significantly more funding was required.

"The way I financed it was I did two little sections first and sold those to MTV and the Tournée of Animation," explains Bill. "That gave me enough money to get started, and then half way through the film I was hired to do a couple commercials. Fortunately that gave me enough money to finish the film without getting outside investment."

On completion, *Tune* made the film festival rounds and received the prestigious Houston WorldFest Gold Jury Special Award and a Spirit Award nomination for Best Film Score.

Bill next moved to live-action with *J. Lyle*, a wacky, surreal comedy about a sleazy lawyer who meets a magical talking dog that changes his life. Soon after, he completed *Guns on the Clackamas*, an imaginary disastrous Western mockumentary. His next animated feature, *I Married a Strange Person*, is a heartwarming story of a newlywed couple on their wedding night. Grant, the husband, starts experiencing strange, supernatural powers and Kerry, his wife, can't cope. Bill considers this film to be most representational of his humor and style.

Bill's next animated feature, *Mutant Aliens*, the story of a stranded astronaut returning to Earth after twenty years in space, won the 2001 Grand Prix in Annecy.

## Hair High

Bill's latest feature film, *Hair High*, is a gothic fifties high school comedy about a love triangle that goes terribly bad when two young, murdered teens return to their prom for revenge.

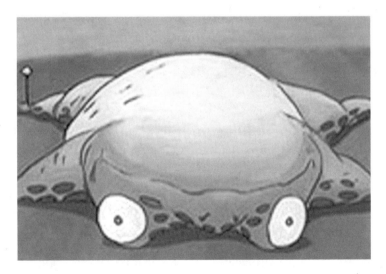

Animation still from *Hair High*.

While he was making *Hair High*, Bill added a wonderful, educational component for students by using the Web to demonstrate the animation process.

"I put a little camera over my drawing board and it was hooked up to the Internet, so everybody in the world could watch me do every single drawing of *Hair High*," explains Bill. "Not only was that fun for me but it was really great for any kind of animation or film students out there to watch how an animated film is drawn from beginning to end.

"A lot of young filmmakers have this concept that just making the film is all there is to it, and they're totally wrong. There are three major stages of having a successful film. The first one, of course, is raising the money, and that blocks a lot of people because if you're going to do a feature film you're talking about $100,000 or at least $50,000, and that's a lot of money. The second stage is making the film itself, and that of course is the fun part, but it's pretty intense. And the third stage, and probably the most important one, is getting the film out there. Getting your investment back. This is really difficult for a lot of people, me included. You have to enter it in all the festivals, you have to market it, you have to get press kits, you have to get a publicity person, you have to do posters, flyers, postcards. You've got to make deals with distributors and make sure they come to the screening, you've got to make sure you don't get screwed on a contract, you've got to make sure when it comes out in movie theaters that it's publicized. So the third stage is really arduous, but a very important part of the process."

## Having a Life

While animation is a laborious, time-consuming process, Bill keeps his priorities in check.

"Not only do you lose perspective in real life but you lose perspective in your film," says Bill. "I try to have a relatively normal life. I hang out with friends and go to a lot of films, parties, screenings, and dinners. I'm basically a party guy and love meeting new people and traveling, so I'm not just this monk sitting at my table and drawing constantly. I think you have to be a real person to survive in this business."

Bill Plympton has found success in one of the most challenging creative fields but truly believes anyone with a strong passion for the craft is capable of the same thing.

"I tell everybody that it's possible to survive as an independent. You just have to really want to do it and you have to really enjoy doing it. If you enjoy doing it, then it's not a job, it's a vacation. At the same time, it's a real leap of faith, like jumping off a cliff without a parachute. Sometimes you land in feathers, and sometimes you land on the rocks. So far I've been lucky to land on feathers."

## Protect Your Project

As Bill mentioned, it is important to protect the rights of your project. Before submitting your film to distributors or others, you should obtain a copyright. A copyright will secure exclusive rights. A work must be original to be copyrighted, so if your film is based on a published book or story, you must have already gained the rights from the owner to use it in such a way. You cannot copyright "ideas" for projects you plan to make in the future. In order to copyright, material must be a tangible, original piece of work.

In the United States, copyright pertaining to the film industry includes the following rights:

▶ *Reproductive Right*: The right to make copies of a work
▶ *Adaptive Right*: The right to produce derivative works based on a copyrighted work
▶ *Distribution Right*: The right to distribute copies of a work
▶ *Performance Right*: The right to perform a copyrighted work in public
▶ *Display Right*: The right to display a copyrighted work in public

You can download a registration from the U.S. Copyright Office's online address at *http://lcweb.loc.gov/copyright/forms.html*. For films and video recordings, order Form PA, Package 110. There is a $20 filing fee.

If you find yourself in a position where you are negotiating your rights with a studio or distributor, these rights come in two forms: *exclusive* and *non-exclusive* rights. Exclusive rights means you cannot promote or sell your project during the time period in which those rights have been agreed to under contract. Non-exclusive rights allow you to seek other markets for your project. More detailed information on your rights in the distribution process can be found in chapter 19.

# CHAPTER 16

# Mission Possible

*"I love documentaries more than feature films because it's real life. It's how you see the world through the filter of your heart and your eyes."*

SHULI ESHEL, ESHEL PRODUCTIONS, CHICAGO

Documentary filmmaker Shuli Eshel.

I first encountered Shuli Eshel of Eshel Productions at a Women in Film meeting in Chicago. It was hard to miss Shuli with her curly red locks, thick Israeli accent, and effervescent buoyancy. Years later we discovered we shared a very dear mutual friend, production designer Katherine Bulovic, who reconnected us for this book.

An Israeli born Chicago filmmaker, Shuli is an award-winning producer/director of videos, films, and documentaries covering a myriad of subjects. From corporate and promotional pieces to socially significant documentaries, she brings a multitude of talent and vision to her art. She is former president of IFP/Midwest, a national organization of independent filmmakers. Shuli has been on the film and television faculties of Columbia College and Roosevelt University in Chicago as well as the Tel-Aviv Museum and College of Design in Israel.

These days she runs a full-service video and film production company and operates Eshel Productions to forward her cinematic mission. Shuli's mission has been to use films as a political tool and make socially conscious documentaries that reflect her view of the world as well as explore cultural and artistic diversity. Her impressive list of documentary credits include:

- *To Be a Woman Soldier–The Role of Women in the Israeli Army*
- *Agam–Creation in Movement, Yaacov Agam's Creation of the Fire-Water Sculpture in Israel*
- *Perception of the "Other"–Exploring Cultural Diversity*
- *Women's Peace in the Middle East*
- *One Step Ahead: Israeli and Palestinian Women–Women in the Forefront of the Peace Effort*
- *Gutman–Life and Work of Israeli Artist Nahum Gutman*
- *Maxwell Street: A Living Memory–The Jewish Experience in Chicago*

Shuli began her career making political spots for the women's movement in Israel and at the same time securing a position as a production assistant with Israeli Television (IBA-Israel Broadcasting Authority), where she eventually directed over a hundred feature stories for a children's magazine program called *What's Up*.

"I produced five-minute feature segments which were short portraits of either an artist or an exhibition," explains Shuli. "I really liked making these shorts. It was good practice and that taught me how to tell a story in a concise way with a beginning, middle, and end within five minutes."

While working at Israeli Television in 1977, Shuli came up with the idea of doing a thirty-minute documentary on abortion and was given the go-ahead.

"That was my first documentary, and it made headlines because abortions were illegal in Israel at the time," recalls Shuli. "The people in the Knesset, Israel's Parliament, heard that the documentary was aired, and they were supposed to vote for or against legal abortion the following week. Since some of the members of the abortion committee did not get to see it, they called Israeli Television and asked if they could have a private screening of the documentary before the voting date. The director of IBA was present and so was I. It was an historical moment for me. We screened the film, and a week later the Knesset members voted for legalizing abortion in Israel. So it was really like, Wow, not many times does a filmmaker get that type of effect doing a documentary! When making the documentary, we used a candid camera and captured the panel of doctors degrading the women as they were grilling them. It was very, very powerful and the film showed how absurd and humiliating the system was when women, married or unmarried, had to plead for their life in order to get an abortion and for the most part were rejected."

## Women in the Middle East

In 1979 Shuli returned to Israel from the United States with a $2,000 donation from U.S./Israel Women to Women to produce an hour-long documentary about the role of women in the Israeli Army. The completed film was the first of its kind on this subject, entitled *To Be a Woman Soldier*, because it exploded the myth of equality between men and women in the Israeli Army. Despite the controversy, or maybe because of it, the film was widely distributed. It was aired on Israeli TV (IBA), purchased by the Israeli Army (IDF), and portions of it were shown on local U.S. broadcasts.

"The success of this film was followed by Israeli TV commissioning me to produce two half-hour specials," says Shuli.

After getting married, Shuli and her husband formed Action Productions in Tel-Aviv, focusing mostly on promotional commercial and industrial projects. A year after the first Intifada, The Palestinian uprising in Israel in 1987, they moved to New York.

"My next project was to make a documentary about the women's point of view in the Middle East conflict," explains Shuli. "I felt that women did not have a platform to express their voice. I also realized that the mainstream media in America was not really showing anything about the involvement and contribution of Israeli women in helping solve the crisis of the 1987 Palestinian uprising. It was very evident that grass roots women's organizations like Women in Black and others, who were very active in paving the road to peace in the Middle East, were left out of the picture. I became very passionate about enabling women to have their voices heard and began raising funds to make a documentary entitled *Women's Peace in the Middle East*. It was tough since I was a newcomer in the United States, in fact an immigrant, and had to undergo a huge cultural adjustment, but I managed to raise $15,000. In December 1999, I took off to Israel to shoot the film. It was a challenge to make the film since I needed to go to the West bank and Gaza to include Palestinian women. But at the time, it was illegal to speak with the PLO (Palestine Liberation Organization), so no one wanted to insure my crew; I took a chance and crossed what is known as the 'green line' (the occupied territories) without insurance and permits by the Israeli authorities. That was a risky thing to do, which I would never do today. Then, I was young and foolish and felt that I could save the world with my films! After five weeks, I came back to Chicago and started editing the film. It ended up being a very powerful document showing the power of women influencing public opinion in a time of crisis. But I was not able to get it shown on Israeli or American TV. However, Habonim, a Jewish Youth Movement organization, offered me a sponsored national tour, showing the documentary at the different Hillel Centers at various universities across the United States. The reaction of the students, mainly Jewish and Arabs at the various campuses, was interesting and at times pretty controversial and heated. Many students had never heard that there were any peace forces in Israel, the West Bank, and Gaza, or that Israeli and Palestinian women were dialoguing and trying to find an alternative way in bridging the differences to pave the road to peace in the Middle East."

## Cultural Diversity

After completing *Women's Peace in the Middle East*, Shuli parted ways with her husband and she moved from New York to Chicago. She remained true to her mission with her next documentary, *Mudpeoples*, about an African-American clay artist.

"I'm interested in the underdog, meaning people who don't get exposure in the media, to try to influence the social structure of where I am, and I realized that there were many black women in Chicago who did not get exposure. I met the president of the Chicago Women's Caucus for Art, Sherry Rabbino, who commissioned me to produce a film about their city wide exhibition called *Perception of the "Other": Exploring Cultural Diversity*. I was very excited because I felt that that was exactly up my alley! I was asked to document the way art helped to bridge the cultural differences in Chicago—White versus Black, young versus old, American versus immigrant, and so forth. One of the women in that documentary was a Black clay artist by the name of Marva Jolly. I was thinking at the time of making a documentary series about women making choices. Marva Jolly was a great inspirational and motivating force, and I decided to begin the series with a documentary about her life. Again, I had to go through the process of raising funds through grants and private donations.

"This time it was easier because my subject was female and African American. Marva created the first all-Black women's collective called Sapphire and Crystal. I made a portrait about Marva Jolly but also included these other women artists in the collective, and it was the first time somebody said that they had ever seen a group of Black women meeting in a basement talking about art. The film got a lot of exposure. It was premiered at the Art Institute of Chicago by then-director of education Ronne Hartfield and later aired on PBS in Chicago.

## Promoting Carol Moseley-Braun

After making *Mudpeoples*, Shuli aggressively sought her next project, this time in the political arena. It was the election year of 1992 and Carol Moseley-Braun was the first African American running for the U.S. Senate. Taking initiative, Shuli wrote to Moseley Braun, introducing herself as a filmmaker and suggesting the creation of a fundraising video.

"I didn't know anyone in the Braun campaign," admits Shuli, "but after sending a cold letter, I got a call from the media consultant who came from Columbus, Ohio. I gave him my demo reel; he liked my work, and I got the job. I was very pleased because I had been in Chicago for less than three years, and I knew I needed a big breakthrough, and this gave me the opportunity of getting into the heart of the democratic machine in Chicago. The project ended up being a thirteen-minute, highly successful coffee video and a TV commercial. The campaign people ordered 1500 copies and distributed it all over the state of Illinois, helping raise funds and electing Carol, as the first African-American woman in the U.S. Senate. Again, I felt I helped make history!"

## Cavalcade Communications Group

With the success of the Moseley-Braun video and *Mudpeoples*, Shuli expected the tide to turn in her favor. However, as the months passed without any new jobs, she grew increasingly worried.

"After the election, I was expecting to get some film work, but nothing came up for a few months. I was teaching film at Columbia College in Chicago but that was very little income, about $600 a month for a few courses, and you cannot live on that. So I thought, Well, I have to start my own company."

In 1993, Shuli collaborated with another Columbia College professor, Roger Schatz, to form Cavalcade Communications Group, a full-service video and film production company. Her partnership agreement included keeping Eshel Productions for documentary projects, while Cavalcade would focus on commercial projects. Cavalcade is now over ten years old.

"I think it is a good thing to have a partner," says Shuli. "However, there are always difficult moments, and at one point when we had an office together I thought I was going to go crazy. I probably would not have continued the partnership had we stayed in the same office. When the lease was over, we decided to work out of our own homes and that gave us both the space and the freedom to work according to our own rhythm. This way you're really like an independent soul, employed by yourself, and you decide on the day and the time you do certain things."

## Maxwell Street: A Living Memory

Shuli's latest project through Eshel Productions is *Maxwell Street: A Living Memory*. The half-hour documentary captures the essence of this once-famous Chicago market through the vivid memories of the children

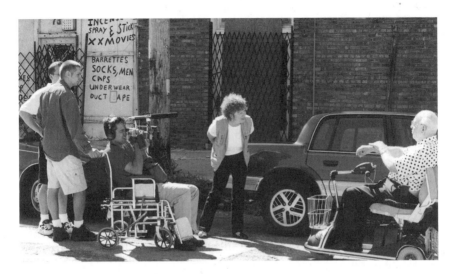

Eshel on location with *Maxwell Street*.

and grandchildren of the Jewish immigrants from Eastern Europe, complemented by rare archival footage and still images. Memories include bargain shopping, the unforgettable aroma of kosher hot dogs and corned beef sandwiches, and the spirituals and blues performed by African Americans who added to the area's special ambiance.

"I've been a pioneer in a sense that I make films about social and political issues and support women and the arts. Many of them have been first or controversial. However, as I am maturing, I have become mellower, and the Maxwell Street project was nice because it was about my heritage and reminded me that my grandparents were also Russian immigrants that moved from Russia to Palestine, and I was an immigrant when I first came to New York in 1988. As a result, I could identify with the struggle of the Jewish immigrants on Maxwell Street."

The project's inception started with a call Shuli received from Elliot Zashin, former director of the Hillel Center of the University of Illinois at Chicago and a treasurer of the Maxwell Street Historic Preservation Coalition. He called Shuli in the summer of 1999 with a request:

"We have not been successful in saving Maxwell Street. Would you be interested in producing a documentary to preserve the memories of some of the Jewish immigrants that created the Maxwell Street market?"

Shuli's answer was an immediate "Yes."

"I knew instinctively that the Jews of Chicago, whom I consider my people, have an important story to tell. I soon realized that the European Jews were fleeing from the pogroms and poverty. They did not speak English, and they were used to a very Jewish way of life. The cultural adjustment was huge as they struggled to survive, raise their children with Jewish values, and give them a good education. In the end, the documentary integrated stories told by these children, providing a context that explained what a Maxwell street background meant in the pursuit of the American dream. Elliot told me that the coalition had received a $1,500 grant from the Illinois Arts Council. Right away, I got a crew and it was very lucky because I interviewed Judge Abraham Lincoln Marovitz (late U.S. district court judge) on his ninety-fourth birthday. It was the last in-depth interview before his death in 2001. He was grateful and touched that we were there. Two and a half years later, with the help of a grant from the Illinois Humanities Council and private donors from the Jewish community, we were able to complete the work. I had raised an additional $12,000 to finish the documentary and the coalition said that since I raised most of the funds, I could own the rights.

"When we premiered the film, we were worried that we would not fill the 440 seats at the auditorium at the Chicago Historical Society. But fortunately, the film touched a nerve in the local community and over 1000 people flocked to see the last remnants of Maxwell Street. We charged $10 per ticket, invited the Maxwell Street Klezmer band to play, showed the film, did a Q&A, and had a catered reception. We ended up offering a second screening to the 300 people or so who were willing to wait an hour. Sadly, in December 2001 they closed off Maxwell Street completely. It was just totally gone. You can't recognize the place now."

Although Maxwell Street is gone, we have not seen the last of Shuli Eshel, who is working on several new documentary projects on the role of Jewish women in American sports and an autobiography that includes her passion for salsa dancing. Her mission, her vision, and her passion are sure to engage and persuade our thinking for years to come.

# CHAPTER 17

# The Balancing Act

*"My wife fell in love with me the night she met me because
I made her laugh. Very often filmmakers have two loves. One
of them is human."*

LES SZEKELY, SECRET'S OUT PRODUCTIONS, CLEVELAND, OH

L es Szekely acknowledges the difficulty of making independent films
on a shoestring. "Saying that filmmaking is kind of challenging is
like saying the Pope is kind of religious," he opines.

Les really has his hands full. In addition to running his company
and hosting the weekly Internet radio show, he is a husband and father
of two. With two kids of my own, I know how hard it is to find balance
between children and work, especially when both are combined into
one space. But whether or not you have a family, finding a balance
between work and personal time is a tough act for any company owner.
It seems that there is always something more to do, whether it is
finishing a client job, writing grants for a new film project, or updating
your company Web site. The boundaries between work and play are
easily blurred.

Before Les was married, he lived in Los Angeles and aspired to
become a screenwriter and filmmaker. He and Gary Rainer, his partner
at the time, were able to get into studios under their company banner
but still ran up against brick walls. With a determination to succeed

combined with creativity and guts, they embarked on one of the funniest schemes I have heard of to get their scripts to the "right people."

"We thought we should go to directors' houses because we weren't
getting anywhere with the 'no' people," explains Les. "But we couldn't
just show up at the door and say we're so-and-so screenwriters. So we
came up with the idea of dressing up like messengers. We even came up
with our own messenger company, Eternal Creek Messenger Service,
and the slogan was "We may be slow but we'll get it there." We printed
signature sheets with a logo and signed phony names in the first ten
slots or so to make it look like it wasn't our first delivery of the day,
which might seem suspicious. We didn't do anything illegal, but we
went to all kinds of folks. I won't mention their names but they're
people you've heard of. We had one blue shirt, so if it was a guy that
I wanted to get to I'd be the messenger and if it was a guy my friend
Gary wanted to get to, we'd switch shirts so he could go. We'd knock
on the door and usually get someone in a uniform or a nice-looking
woman, whether Mrs. So-and-So or not, but sometimes the actual guy
came out. I wanted to say, 'I'm not a messenger, I'm a scriptwriter and
you want to read this!' But we kept our cool. The sad part of the story
is that it never led to anything, but what did we have to lose? We
weren't hurting anyone. If someone walks up to my house, I'll open the
door and if I don't want them in, I'll close the door, simple as that."

When starting out in Los Angeles, Les had little balance between
work and play.

"Are you kidding?" laughs Les. "I was completely insulated. It was
my entire life. If you have all your eggs in this one basket of trying to
make it in filmmaking, you will go nuts. There were nights when I was
cursing, upset, and angry. Thank goodness I now have my family
because it really gave me balance. It made me discover there is something else. Filmmaking is great but there's this whole other life that's
more important. I'm also a musician, and one night before I met my
wife I got a new drum machine. I had a date with a young woman and
I was showing it to her. She left the room and I heard her come back
and say, 'Hey, turn around.' She was wearing practically nothing and
smiling at me. I looked at her and said, 'Give me one more minute with
this drum machine.' Band practice and filmmaking was number one

with me. We got into a big fight that night, and I haven't seen her in a very, very long time. That's how ridiculously insulated I was."

## Becoming Mr. Cleaver

Les recently moved his company and family to his hometown of Cleveland to offer his children a "normal" life around family and friends.

"I may be John Carpenter at night but I'm Ward Cleaver during the day," jokes Les. "The last film I did, *I Know What You Did in English Class*, is a film that took me the longest to make. Before that I'd shoot something, edit nonstop, twenty-four hours a day for a couple months. You can ask my lovely wife about the many dates we did not go on because of that. Once the kids came, a lightening bolt hit me and I encourage any filmmaker to get caught up in that spark. I almost missed my daughter's second birthday party because we were shooting a film and my wife said, 'Honey, I love you, but are you out of your mind? Think about what you're doing.' I listened to her and thought about it and said, 'You know, you're absolutely right.' So I left shoot early. From that point on I've been the same ever since.

"I don't want to wake up one day, not know my kids, and only see somebody in my house who's got blue hair with half of it shaved off. And this is, of course, while the police officer is telling me they've been arrested. That's not going to be me. I'm not the stereotypical dad. If you ask me when my daughter's choir concert is, I don't say I don't know. Are you kidding? I know the date, the time, the place, and the car I'm going to use to get there. I'm very family oriented and I do not let this take a back seat. This is why it took me so long to make this last film."

Over the years, Les has made a number of low-budget comedic horrors, such as *Vampire Time Travelers*, *The Not So Grim Reaper*, *Night of the Living Date*, and *I Know What You Did in English Class*.

"*The Not So Grim Reaper* is like *Spinal Tap* meets death," says Les of one of his projects. "It's shot like a documentary of a day in the life of the Grim Reaper. A filmmaker follows the Grim Reaper, who shows him how he handles different deaths. My last film, *I Know What You Did in English Class*, was made simply to be made. What happens with it now, only the future will tell."

Les's love of filmmaking is obvious, as he continues to make movies without funding or worrying too much about marketing or distribution. He is doing it out of sheer pleasure. His love for his family is equally obvious, and he has found the necessary balance to enjoy both of his passions.

"I love filmmaking but if I don't know my family as a result of it, what's the point?"

## A Sideline Venture

Unlike most other filmmakers in this book, Les's production company is a part-time venture, not a full-time job. Thus, he doesn't have to worry about generating a substantial income from the company in order to make a living. This is certainly a viable way to start a company, especially if you have a lot of financial obligations. Like most other filmmakers in this book, he has branched into commercial and video production, which he offers under a subcompany to separate it from his creative work.

"Secret's Out Productions has a separate arm called Creative Videos for television commercials, weddings, and other things," Les explains. "I call it Creative Videos because if somebody reads Secret's Out Productions they might go, *What*? I've been fortunate since I've been back in Cleveland. A lot of folks that I knew as a child have started their own businesses so I've made commercials for them. And I'm becoming more and more successful at it because I'm doing these things with a filmmaking background and a lot of experience in shoestring budgets. People don't believe the budgets I come up with because they're used to much higher numbers. But over the course of time I've become a one-man show. I've literally traveled with my editing system on my lap in airplanes. It's a way to support the company."

## The Truth about Self-Employment

For those who choose to make a production company a full-time venture, it helps to understand some of the myths versus realities involved. I have discovered that people who are employed by others confuse "self-employed" with "comfortably unemployed," as if we have all the time in the world to get involved in their causes. Without a nine-to-five commitment, they assume we are free to fundraise, join PTA committees, assist on independent projects, organize events, and hang out on their lunch breaks.

This illusion is largely due to false advertising about the incredible freedom you will enjoy from being your own boss. The truth is there is nothing more challenging and time-consuming than managing your own company. You may be president, but in most cases you are also head of the production, marketing, accounting, IT, shipping and receiving, and housekeeping departments, to name a few. And then there is working long hours on sets, generating an income, and collecting payment on past-due invoices while your bills are stacking up. Frey Hoffman of Freydesign Productions struggled to find a balance in the early years.

"Starting off, especially when you're young and eager to get working in the industry, your personal life can become obliterated," he says. "It can virtually disappear because all of your time is spent working on films. It doesn't have to be a major production to still require fifteen-hour days, day in and day out. Having family and friends is a process that takes a lifetime but the proximity of people that you work with on a production makes them start feeling like your family and friends, though more by circumstance than choice. It's definitely important to make that distinction and to find a place for family and friends that exist outside of the industry."

Like Frey and Les, I was a complete workaholic when I started my company in the early nineties. On top of working insane hours for various clients, pulling all-nighters to get scripts finished on time, and networking like mad to get more clients, I also had an infant son. My husband at the time was home during the day, and the moment I entered the door he deposited our baby into my arms. I cringe at my feelings of utter frustration and resentment about never having any time to myself. The only one I should have resented was me, as I had built my own world and did have the power to change my circumstances.

Eventually I learned to use the invaluable word "no" and it didn't ruin my life. As in "no" to working for free on independent projects, "no" to volunteering for filmmaking groups, "no" to joining friends at unnecessary social functions, and so forth. After all, didn't I start my own company to be independent and have flexibility to spend time with the people I loved? In retrospect, using the word "no" was one of the best decisions I ever made.

There are plenty of other myths surrounding self-employment, including:

▶ You have to have certain personality traits to succeed, such as being aggressive or business-oriented.
▶ Self-employment is too risky if you don't have a lot of cash at the outset.
▶ Self-employment causes people to become very isolated.
▶ People won't take you seriously if you work out of your house.
▶ As a home business, you won't be able to compete with bigger production companies in your area.
▶ Only a lucky few succeed at self-employment.

It can be difficult to separate myths from reality, especially if others use them to question what you are attempting to do. The best thing to do is look at the huge number of filmmakers who have found success in starting their own companies. And success is only a matter of how you define it. For those like Les Szekely, it's being able to do what you love without losing sight of the importance of family and friends. *What is important to you*?

# PART IV

# PROMOTING YOUR COMPANY

# CHAPTER 18

# Marketing Strategies

*"It's like a domino effect; someone gets your card and likes it, then they check out your Web site and that's consistent and still within what they're looking for, then they pick up the phone. The more all of these things mesh, the better."*

JAMEY BRUMFIELD, YOUR PLAN B

No company finds success without spreading the word about its products and services, directed to the right target audience. This holds true for film production company owners (assuming you want to make a living at your craft) as you need to get attention for your specific projects and, if applicable, your production services.

Effective marketing does not mean you have to spend a fortune on advertising or direct mail. Many filmmakers find publicity opportunities through press releases, film screenings, at film festivals and networking events, and through the Internet. At the same time, filmmakers often neglect to include marketing and promotion in their budgets, whether for a specific film or overall company expenses.

Typically, 10 to 25 percent of a film budget is devoted to marketing and promotion. This varies depending on the size of the budget. Hollywood studio films might spend a considerably higher percentage on "hot" theatrical releases while low-budget independents with very limited resources may have less available. Some producers, especially those working on low-budget independents, opt to do their own marketing, while others use entertainment marketing specialists. There are pros and cons to both approaches. Entertainment marketing specialists are not cheap, but they do have experience in promotion. Always get a referral and review their background if you are considering this option.

"When you don't have a marketing background, you are going to make mistakes, period," says Joni Brander of Brander Broadcast Consulting. "Marketing is overwhelming. When I started my company I did a mass mailing to TV stations and then did the follow-up calls, and people would say I didn't get it, can you send it again. Sometimes they would say that three times! When you do this by yourself, redoing mailings is a big deal. Basically, you're going to make a lot of mistakes, and one of mine was sending materials out generically and blindly as opposed to calling first and getting an idea of their interest, so they would be expecting it."

If you are not using an entertainment marketing specialist, the producer of your project—whether that is you or someone you hire to do the job—should come on board with a marketing strategy and a good understanding of your target audience. Why will audiences want to see this film? Will your film play well domestically, either in theaters or on home video? Is it suited for the international market? What public relations, sales agents, or distribution companies are best suited to help promote your projects?

Film production company owners have to market two components: their companies and their specific film projects.

## Marketing and Promoting Your Company

Marketing a company means branding an image and promoting products and services. Like the films you make, your company needs to be defined by visuals and words that should appear on everything you create, from business cards and letterhead to Web sites and promotional products.

"You want to pick a color that represents your company and use it on everything," suggests Jamey Brumfield of Your Plan B, a Web development and marketing company in Chicago. "We use lime green and it's everywhere. We like to be playful because we figure everybody is working, working, working so we do a big holiday time mailing with little toys and treats, all green of course. Some people like to do that for Easter or Cinco de Mayo or St. Patrick's Day. If everything in your company is pastels, I would send out something in April and play up the spring aspect of life."

Many companies use logos in addition to a color scheme. Jamey believes it is important to have a logo with a life span of at least two to four years.

"You never know how long anyone will hold onto your business card, and you don't want them to have a card that's a year old while your site's completely different."

"Also, make sure the logo looks good small or you have a small version available," adds Your Plan B partner David Birdwell. "You can have a fancy four-color 3-D logo but you want to design it so that when it's photocopied on your fax letterhead at half an inch it still looks good."

Many filmmakers are reluctant to invest in marketing and promotional tools as there is rarely direct evidence of how much income these methods generate in terms of jobs or sales.

"You have to think of every tool as part of your whole arsenal," says Jamey. "I don't think any one thing is going to grab someone enough to say, 'I'm hiring you today.' You can have the coolest business card, and they're still going to want to talk to you on the phone or check out your Web site. At, very least you need a business card that you can leave with people. Letterhead, fax, and envelopes should be consistent with the card. Your voicemail message also has to reflect your company. We're currently working with an up-and-coming film director, and his cell phone message is so creative, you're not sure if you really got him or not. If someone calls you, you want them to know they reached the right number."

## Company Web Site

One of the most important marketing tools is a company Web site. The mistake that many people make is to think that putting up a Web site will automatically generate business; it will not. People generally do not go to a Web site to conduct business unless they already know about the company (the likelihood of your company being hired because a distributor or a CEO discovered you while idly surfing the Web is almost nil). However, while the site may not result in actual revenue, it is, in essence, your company portfolio or media kit to which you can refer prospective investors, producers, distributors, and so forth. While many filmmakers are savvy Web site designers, others, like me, are not and must rely on a professional.

"When selecting a Web site designer you want to look at what he's done," advises Jamey. "You want to make sure he's going to work quickly for you and that he's going to be there when you call. I would look for testimonials and see how long the designer has been in business. You really want to see examples of what he's made, because if it's all front-page templates in different colors, he's not really being a designer."

Fortunately, prices for getting a domain name have been steadily dropping from two to four hundred dollars in 1997 down to ten or twenty dollars today. An affordable professional Web site designer typically charges $1,500 to $3,000, depending on the number of pages and creative elements.

"You can always find it more expensive or cheaper based on who you know or timing," says Jamey. "One hint is that the Web business is slower in the summer so sometimes you can get better deals then. It's not as busy as the fall because everyone's working through their budgets. We tell a lot of people that come to us with a limited budget that if they can wait until the summer then we'll be happy to work on their site at a reduced rate."

Filmmakers just starting their own companies may be reluctant to spend significant dollars on professional designs and opt for free or affordable templates, at least at the beginning.

"I know all about not having a budget to jump out there and do a big marketing campaign," Jamey empathizes. "If you've got your domain name and you can make a very simple Web site just to get something going, that's fine. But down the road, there's going to be a point where somebody will look at your Web site and know they saw four other sites that look exactly alike. It's the same with using too much stock photography or clip art."

Frey Hoffman of Freydesign Productions concurs.

"I'm determined to not put up anything on the Web that's not first-rate. It really becomes your public face. Sometimes you meet someone who actually checks out your Web site and when they find you, you want to make sure you look your best."

Jamey and David have seen the good, the bad, and the ugly of Web site layouts and offer their 'do and don'ts':

Do

- ▶ Make your Web site printer friendly, as it may get printed by an assistant rather than by the person who actually wants the information.
- ▶ Make your Web site easy to navigate.
- ▶ Test your Web site on multiple browser settings and desktop configurations.
- ▶ Use bigger, easy-to-read, non-serif fonts because fancy fonts can be hard to read, especially if they're small.
- ▶ Pick a theme and stick with it. It will only benefit you.
- ▶ Filmmakers and other creative types should avoid navy blue, because it is a standard corporate business color. Choose a more dynamic color.
- ▶ Since the Internet is changing into a giant phone book, make your contact information very easy to access.
- ▶ Add interactive or moving elements for visual stimulation.
- ▶ Showcase your work on your Web site–it's cheaper than sending out DVDs and tapes.
- ▶ Update your Web site often enough to keep it fresh.

Don't

- ▶ Your Web site is not a refrigerator where you want to add everything you ever made. Showcase your finer moments, not everything down to what you made in film school.
- ▶ Unless you are making a Web site for the Pirates of the Caribbean, try not to make it a treasure hunt of where to get information. Easy navigation is key!
- ▶ Don't include everything on the homepage. Think of the homepage as Cliff's Notes to your company and save the detailed information for other pages.

▶ Don't add personal information on the site. People who don't know you are not interested in your cat or beach vacation, and it makes you appear unprofessional.

▶ Don't add extras you don't need, such as guest books or counters, unless they are relevant to your site and target audience.

▶ Don't use clip art and stock photography if you want to look unique, which you do!

One of Your Plan B's tips is to add an interactive component.

"Because you're in the film or multimedia industry, you want to play with that on your Web site," says Jamey. "Either have an integrated flash element or some little sound or movement in the top third of your screen. It helps people keep reading your page if they see a slight movement. You don't want to see something that's blinking because that gets annoying. But a subtle movement or a transition of colors or images coming and going helps make it fresher. And you're explaining to your user immediately that you do moving pictures. It's a subconscious thing."

"It's good to have an interface design," agrees David. "Like when the user rolls over a button or text, it colors and they know to click on it for more details."

"As far as updates, you don't have to update your Web site every single day or month," Jamey says of one of their other tips. "But you want to make sure that you have the illusion that you're keeping the site current. You can do that by using online tools like Blog or Live Journal, where you can log in and type in some news or updates. Or you can use a tool where you add about six months of little blurbs and they are automatically added to your site on given dates. If you keep your Web site current, even in little ways, it gives the illusion that you're giving it a lot of attention. There are other things you can do. Let's say that you've got fifteen really great photos from one of your film shoots. You can set it up with a java script tool so that every time a user sees your home page they see one of those fifteen photos, but not necessarily the same one every time. That simple tool gives the illusion that you're changing something, even though it's a set bank of photos."

Once you have a Web site up and running, how do you attract people to your site? Listing it on search engines with good meta tags is crucial, say the Your Plan B partners. It is also important to add the site to print pieces that you drop off or mail.

"You want it to become part of your signature for everything you do, from sending e-mails to any articles you write," says David.

## Word of Mouth

Jerry Vasilatos uses a Web site as one tool for promoting Nitestar Productions. He also has a director's and an editor's reel on easy-to-ship DVD copies, as well as promotional flyers, which he regularly sends out to a production company list he has compiled over the years. Still, he finds that most opportunities come through word of mouth.

"When I first got my Avid system, I spent a lot of money on advertising in industry magazines," Jerry recalls. "Frankly, it was a waste of money as, so far, most of my business has come from referrals."

## Contact Lists

Getting referrals can be difficult when you start out. In the early stages of owning a company, it is important to research your potential clients and compile a database that you can use to log phone calls you have made, mailings you have sent out, follow-up calls, and so forth. Georgina Willis and Kerry Rock created a filing system to keep track of contacts and players in the industry.

"We keep our own database on who's doing what, where, and when," explains Kerry. "You read things but don't necessarily take them in so we keep a series of files with a lot of stuff that we can refer to. So if we hear about a certain company that's doing something, we can quickly refer to file and say, Okay that's the deal behind that."

The ease and speed of the Internet has certainly opened up networking opportunities and provides an easy method for staying in touch with contacts.

"Most people prefer to read an e-mail than play phone tag with somebody," says Joni Brander. "E-mail is a great way to market and keep relationships going and is much easier than the phone. And, again, this is long-term stuff that you're building over years so you are top of mind when the need comes up."

One effective way to start your contact list is to collect business cards at networking events. Mailing lists are also an option.

"If you have built an advertising or marketing budget into your company, it's very important to get hold of mailing lists, such as through the Hollywood Creative Directory, to find production companies to which you can send out your demo reel or literature about your company," Jerry Vasilatos advises.

The Hollywood Creative Directory (production company listings) and a number of other useful directories can be found at *www.hcdonline.com*.

## Direct Mail

If you do a direct mailing, it is important to make it visually memorable. Jim Machin of R.duke Productions in Chicago came up with a unique strategy that certainly caught people's eyes.

"I sent out nude pictures of myself with a camera over my critical area and the mailer said, 'You want the stripped down package?' It was pretty successful. People would recognize me as the nude guy with the camera, so at least they remembered who I was!"

## Press Releases

Many filmmakers use press releases as a free way to promote their companies. The ideal time to send press releases out is when a specific event is happening, such as going into production with an exciting new project, winning a film festival award, or contributing your time on a production for a nonprofit organization. Publications rarely print articles from press releases that look too promotional or self-serving, so it must be written in such a way that looks enticing, informational, and pertinent to readers. Supplying photos is always a plus. There are a number of books and resources for writing effective press releases. For example, *Writing Effective News Releases . . .: How to Get Free Publicity for Yourself, Your Business, or Your Organization* by former reporter Catherine McIntyre (Piccadilly Books, 1992) is a practical guide that contains plenty of examples to help you start your PR campaign the right way.

You want the stripped down package?

## Marketing Specific Film Projects

Most filmmakers aspire for theatrical release, but it is important to recognize that only about 400 films play in U.S. theaters each year, and most of these are big budget studio features.

Marketing a film, documentary, or animation requires finding the right audience and gaining their interest in your project. To understand the marketplace you must get to know potential buyers, which is most easily done at film festivals where buyers are in surplus and have knowledge about who can best distribute and promote your particular projects.

There are a number of tools that filmmakers use to promote their independent projects, including:

- ► Film trailers
- ► Publicity kits
- ► Movie posters
- ► Press releases

### Film Trailers

Film trailers are used to secure funding or find distribution opportunities. Just like the trailers that precede theatrically released films, your trailer needs to excite and entice your audience into wanting to see more. There is a skill to cutting trailers, so if you are not experienced at doing them, find an editor who is.

One example of a successful film in which a trailer was used to raise production costs is *Blood Simple*, written and directed by Joel and Ethan Coen, better known as the Coen Brothers. In 1991 they made a 35-mm trailer that showed gunshots piercing a wall with light filtering through the holes, as well as a scene of a man being buried alive. Rather than go to the studios, they approached Hadassah, the Women's Zionist Organization of America, which is committed to promoting the unity of the Jewish people. They were able to get a list of the one hundred wealthiest Jews in Minnesota (their home state) and solicited them one by one, showcasing their trailer to gain the financing they needed to complete the film. The final budget they raised was $750,000 through Hadassah and $550,000 from sixty-eight other investors.

### Publicity Kits

Publicity (or press) kits are used to generate interest in your film from the media and may contain a DVD copy of your trailer, if available. They are handed out at press screenings and sent to industry publications. Given the amount of material that editors receive, it is very important to make a good first impression.

A publicity kit usually includes:

- Cover letter (describing why the editor should want to review your project)
- Project synopsis
- Cast list
- Producer, director, cinematography, and composer bios
- Production stills (usually black-and-white 8″ × 10″ glossies)
- Fact sheet (genre, running time, film medium, etc.)
- Movie poster or postcard
- Trailer (on DVD if possible)
- Relevant articles and press releases
- Contact information

## Film Festivals

Although you want your film seen, some experts recommend against overexposure, or your film might start to look like used goods. The best festivals, where serious industry players show up with checkbooks, are the larger, reputable venues such as Sundance, Cannes, the AFI festival, Telluride, and Berlin.

One of the biggest networking events in the United States is the American Film Market (AFM), which annually attracts more than 7000 film and industry professionals from around the globe to the Los Angeles event. The eight-day market brings together over 300 motion picture companies and a slew of acquisition and development executives, producers, distributors, agents, attorneys, buyers, and film financiers, and, naturally, independent filmmakers. Hundreds of films that are completed or still in production find financing and packaging at this event.

Screening at the Sundance Film Festival is every independent filmmaker's dream. Created by Robert Redford as part of the Sundance Institute in Utah, this festival is internationally recognized as a showcase for the best in new American independent film.

The Cannes Film Festival, or Festival de Cannes, is the most preeminent European stage for screening independent films. Feature and short films from around the globe are selected for Official Competition,

Out of Competition, and Un Certain Regard sections. All first feature films are eligible for the coveted Camera d'Or.

Prior to attending any of these or other festivals, filmmakers need to promote, publicize, and advertise their projects. In other words, create a buzz by building hype in publications and word of mouth so that audiences will have a desire to see your film.

An excellent model of hype is *The Blair Witch Project*. The filmmakers created an eight-minute trailer that made it look as though the project was an actual documentary, not fiction. They mounted small posters around the Cannes Film Festival, again implying that the film's subject was based on real events. The Web site they created also gave the same implication. Once Artisan Entertainment picked up the picture, they wouldn't let any of the talent give interviews to continue the myth that the filmmakers were actually dead. We all know the explosive results of that film.

Of course you don't want to build false hype so that your screening becomes a letdown compared to expectations. It is the old, subtle act of seduction where the performance must be worth the tease.

There are countless resources that provide film festival links and information on how to best approach such events to your advantage. For example, *The Ultimate Film Festival Survival Guide, 3rd Edition* by Chris Gore (Lone Eagle Publishing Company, 2004) offers information for marketing and selling your films at Sundance, Telluride, Slamdance, and over 400 other festivals worldwide. *MovieMaker Magazine* has a Web site with a comprehensive listing of U.S. and international film festival links at *www.moviemaker.com/festivals.html*. You should also check out your city and/or state film office for useful links and state festivals.

## Movie Posters

Posters are used by filmmakers to promote their films and are often replicated on postcards and newspaper ads. With limited space, visuals and text need to be dramatic and powerful enough to entice an audience. If you end up getting distribution, the distributor may create new artwork for the project, depending on the promotional strategies the company uses.

The poster for *Boys Don't Cry* shows what appears to be a teenage boy walking down a road, although the face is partially cut off. The text reads, "A true story about finding the courage to be yourself." *She's Gotta Have It* calls itself "a seriously sexy comedy." The *Fargo* poster shows a dead body face down in the snow with the text, "a homespun murder story." The *American Beauty* poster has a naked woman's navel and a rose with the two word tease, "Look closer."

When Jerry Vasilatos made his first indepdent film *Solstice* about a man reevaluating his life on the solstice after a relationship breakup, he designed a poster that shows the main character walking alone down a snow-covered Chicago street with the text, "For some people, the coldest, loneliest night of the year falls on Christmas Eve." This poster's artwork and theme truly capture the essence of the film.

Looking at existing movie posters will help stimulate ideas. Unless you are skilled in graphic design, you should have an experienced designer create your poster, based on the images and words you want to convey. Consider the following questions to help brainstorm layout and wording ideas.

*Solstice* promotional poster.
(© 2004 Nitestar Productions,
all rights reserved.)

▶ What are the key concepts in my film?

▶ What is the underlying theme?

▶ What adjectives best describe the mood and events?

▶ What is the point of highest conflict?

▶ How will audiences emotionally react?

▶ What is the most powerful visual?

▶ Are there subtle, recurring images that are important thematically?

▶ What scenery or location is most representative of my film?

▶ How important is it to show the main character or villain?

▶ What differentiates the look and feel of my film?

## Press Releases for Specific Film Projects

As with promoting your company, press releases provide a great way to get free publicity for specific projects. The trick is to write an effective release with a hook and interesting supporting photos so that an editor is tantalized into running the story. In a sense, you pitch the making of your project to the press in the same way you would pitch a project to development executives, investors, or distributors, though in a way that satisfies the press' readership.

When Jerry Vasilatos directed a *Blair Witch* spoof called *The Blair Witch Rejects*, he created a press release to highlight the project as well as the new distribution arm of his company. He utilized quotes, facts, and a timely subject (the *Blair Witch* craze) to solicit attention.

**JANUARY 14, 2000**

**FOR IMMEDIATE RELEASE:**

**NITESTAR PRODUCTIONS™ LAUNCHES HOME VIDEO LABEL**

**WITH PREMIERE RELEASE "THE BLAIR WITCH REJECTS"**

(LOS ANGELES, CA.) Nitestar Productions™ launched its own home video distribution arm this week with their premiere release, *The Blair Witch Rejects*, a feature length straight to video comedy spoof directed by award winning filmmaker Jerry Vasilatos (*Solstice*, *A Christmas Story*, Lifetime Television). In the very first feature length spoof of *The Blair Witch Project*, *The Blair Witch Rejects* chronicles the misadventures of an inept Beverly Hills independent producer who believes she can ride the coat-tails of the original movie's success by filming a follow-up.

Casting a talented ensemble cast featuring Kevin Leadingham, Chanda Willis, Brent Beebe, Deborah Wolff and others, Jerry Vasilatos approached the film as a satire on independent filmmakers. Using similar preparation techniques as the directors of *Blair Witch* Mr. Vasilatos guided his actors by only providing snippets of their character motivations and plot points as the shoot progressed over three days right up to the surprise ending, this time played for laughs.

"There were several independent groups here in L.A. all jumping on the *Blair Witch* bandwagon shooting their own versions as quickly as they could to cash in on the original's success." Vasilatos says. "To me, that's what was spoofable . . . filmmakers haphazardly rushing to ride the coat-tails of something else, unable to come up with their own original ideas, so that became the focus. We all loved the original *Blair Witch Project*, and witnessing other people rushing to emulate it is what inspired us to poke fun at them instead. The whole thing became a slapstick farce."

Founding their video distribution arm in 1999 with the intention of releasing films and other projects that are developed and produced in-house, Nitestar Productions™ will also focus on reviewing outside independently produced features for release on their new home video label.

*The Blair Witch Rejects* (Color/Unrated/90 Minutes) is now available through Nitestar Home Video™. If you are a press or wholesale contact interested in receiving a screening copy and press kit, please contact Nitestar Productions™ by telephone at 323-468-8089 or by e-mail through this link.

## Press Screenings

Press screenings are a great way to get advance publicity for your film, assuming reviewers offer more praise than criticism. Whether your distributor organizes these events or you do so yourself, you definitely want to host it in a screening room with good projection and sound.

Marketing and promotion takes a huge amount of planning and work but is worth the effort in the long run. After all, what is the point of making your incredible projects if no one sees them? The more you can commit your energy to this critical side of managing a company, the more tangible the benefits you will eventually receive.

# CHAPTER 19

# The Art of Distribution

*"Once you get an agent or distributor it does not take away the need to promote. You have to continue, if not more so, to promote your film and get exposure."*

RUBEN DUA, AMAZE FILMS, LOS ANGELES

**M**any independent filmmakers, especially those just starting out, are intimidated by the distribution and marketing process because it has nothing to do with filmmaking itself. There is a saying in Hollywood that the problem with movies as an art form is that movies are a business, and the problem with movies as a business is that they are an art form. Regardless, entertainment products need to be sold by people who are in touch with the customer and all of the nuances of the purchasing decision. To get their work seen, filmmakers need distributors who are very involved at all levels of the business and take a vested interest in their projects.

Films are typically distributed through major studios or independent distributors, although some filmmakers choose the option of self-distribution. Each approach has advantages and disadvantages.

## Studio Distribution

Distribution through a major studio is the most coveted, as significant financing can be obtained for marketing and distribution (and sometimes development, production, and/or completion funds), ensuring a project gets wide visibility. It also provides the only likely chance for a theatrical release. At the same time, the studio will acquire most of the rights associated with your film.

If a studio agrees to fund your project from beginning to end, you will first be required to sign a development or "step" deal. The memo outlines the agreement, salary, time frames, screen credits, and percentage points. In the deal, the studio agrees to finance the development and/or distribution of the project but can terminate the deal (and not have to pay you any additional money) at any "step" along the way.

Of course, studio deals can be lucrative if you have a captivating project. The most successful independent film to acquire studio financing is *The Blair Witch Project*, which was made for $35,000 and sold to Artisan for $1.1 million (including worldwide rights). The sequel was funded with $18 million.

## Online Distribution

Online distribution, in which films are showcased and sold through the Internet, is a relatively new phenomenon. Online distribution sites funded by studios, existing distributors, and production companies obviously offer benefits and worldwide exposure, although the success of online-only film distribution companies is still under scrutiny. An advantage is that these companies typically offer nonexclusive agreements that are not binding.

## Independent Distributors

As the chances of a studio distribution deal are slim, most filmmakers opt to launch their work through an independent distributor. Since these distributors may not be affiliated with a major studio, they cannot provide the same financial resources for promoting your project and rarely offer financing up front. The advantage of independent distributors is that you tend to get a better percentage and more personalized attention. Keep in mind that hundreds of distribution companies go in and out of business every year. Learning about an independent distributor's track record and years in business will only benefit you.

Probably the most comprehensive distributor listing is the Hollywood Distributors Directory, which is updated once a year. This directory lists detailed information (including individual names, phone/fax, and e-mail addresses) on over 800 domestic and international distribution companies, sales agents, producer and distributor reps, financing companies, film festivals, and more. Information on the guide is available at *www.hcdonline.com*.

I had the pleasure of speaking with two very distinguished independent distributors for this book–Ruben Dua of Amaze Films in Los Angeles and educational/documentary distributor Chip Taylor of Chip Taylor Communications.

Together, they bring a broad, knowledgeable perspective on the distribution process for various types of media and have a good understanding of filmmaker and distributor relationships, as well as typical distribution contracts and royalty issues.

## The Distributor's Perspective

Ruben Dua worked in film production for a number of years when he realized there was a niche for packaging independent short films in a distinct way. He created Amaze Films in 2002 to produce and distribute independent short films, feature films, and the highly acclaimed "Short Series," featuring cult favorites, Sundance/Cannes Film Festival selections, and Academy Award-winning short films on eight short film compilation DVDs. Amaze Films also has an exclusive contract with Akimbo, a premier Internet-based television content provider of high-quality movies, documentaries, music videos, and other video on-demand programming.

"We like films that have received acclaim because that gives an increased perceived value and makes it more desirable for viewers," says Ruben. "On the subjective side, we're looking for films that break ground, explore new subject matter, or touch upon new ideas and stories that haven't been done before. It's also nice to see familiar faces or films that touch on current events or issues taking place in our world that people can relate to."

In the early 1970s Chip Taylor was an elementary school teacher. He then spent ten years working for Journal Films, a pioneering educational film distributor of the day. After the company owner died, Chip began his own distribution company, Apropos Studios, officially changed to Chip Taylor Communications in 1985. Chip takes great pride in his company's slate of offerings and often says "our company doesn't just sell DVD or video, we sell content."

As well as distributing more than 2000 educational and documentary programs, Chip has independently produced over 130 programs. He offers programming in DVD, digital streaming, and various video formats. His gravitation toward education came at a young age.

"When I grew up in a poor neighborhood in Fitchburg, Massachusetts, I saw prejudice against Puerto Rican kids for no other reason than they didn't speak English very well," Chip recalls. "Being a Protestant kid in a mostly Catholic neighborhood, I also experienced prejudice for reasons I didn't understand, from kids and adults alike. I had no father, my mother was very poor, and I started working part-time at thirteen doing janitorial work. It made me realize the only way to get ahead was to get an education, which I eventually did, graduating from Fitchburg State College to become a teacher. The first films I produced were about Puerto Rico. I went there to see what Puerto Ricans were like and found them to be like people everywhere. These programs led me to acquire multicultural programs, and I was one of the first distributors to offer programs showing that America's strength is in its diversity."

Chip seeks programs that meet current educational needs and reflect his artistic passion.

"With my teaching background I always look to distribute programs that are going to help educators teach, especially programs that match curricula standards for teachers. These programs are never to replace a teacher but to aid the teacher and guide the student through audio-visual means. I also love art and have had the great honor to distribute the exclusive biography of Andrew Wyeth, America's most-loved living realist artist. Success with this program has allowed me to produce and acquire programs on many other excellent artists, including Thomas Hart Benton, Fritz Scholder, and just recently I produced three biographies on Edna Hibel, Pierre H. Matisse (the grandson on Henri), and Peter de La Fuente (the great nephew of Andrew Wyeth and grandson of Peter Hurd)."

## Company Distribution versus Self-Distribution

Several filmmakers in this book self-distribute their projects, such as animator Bill Plympton and documentary maker Shuli Eshel. There are advantages and disadvantages to working with distributors, and every filmmaker should spend time exploring their options before making a distribution decision.

"You should never sign a deal without getting it checked," warns Kerry Rock of Potoroo Films. "You can read something and have no idea what it really means, especially the first few times you look at a distribution contract. It is overwhelming. You really need to find a good solicitor who knows the language."

"A lot of filmmakers are very wary of working with distributors because they think they're going to get exploited, but unfortunately the only way to survive for a lot of distribution companies is by retaining most of the profits," says Ruben. "The reality is that with marketing costs and expenses, it's difficult for distribution companies to stay around. So filmmakers have to decide if they're after exposure or money, and once they decide what they're after, they have to seek a deal that accommodates that goal. There are some companies that will give you all the exposure in the world but you'll never see a dime, and for some filmmakers that's a dream. They're not interested in the money; they're interested in showing off their work and getting a picture deal in the future. Other filmmakers just want to make money and often decide to self-distribute, which has been very successful for a lot small production companies. They'll come out with a little sci-fi spoof and sell 10,000 copies through their Web site, make a few bucks, and get some good exposure. I think filmmakers really need to realize exactly what they're after, and once they do, go out and seek it out."

Shuli Eshel of Eshel Productions self-distributes all of her documentary projects. Her recent documentary, *Maxwell Street*, is her biggest financial success to date.

"I made a brochure and did a big mailing," she explains. "Quite soon I sold over 600 copies. The video is also sold at the museum shop of the Chicago Historical Society, and I also receive money from screenings at different museums and organizations. I charge different prices for colleges and libraries and private people, but so far it has done very well."

The biggest advantage of a company distributor is avoiding the expense and time of marketing and promotion.

"Producers usually want to produce," says Chip. "Self-distribution takes time, energy, and money. A good distributor takes over all the distribution tasks, and it should cost the producer no money to get their projects out there, opening time for a producer to move ahead to get more money to make more projects. Distribution is not easy. It's a lot of work, and it does cost money. We do all the art work for our producers' programs, simultaneously release the programs on DVD and video, write and send the press releases, get the project on the Internet within a few days, get it reviewed as quickly as possible, and have it in the hands of our salespeople immediately. A producer should expect that from a quality distributor. We also report our sales and royalties to the producer on a bi-annual basis, which is a standard. No producer should wait longer than six months to hear the results of a program."

## Distribution Agreements

Amaze Films offers non-exclusive agreements while Chip Taylor Communications offers exclusive ones. Both arrangements have their merits.

"We have a revenue sharing deal whereby the series or films we sell, the filmmaker makes money," explains Ruben. "It's typical with short films because there's such a plethora of them out there and the commercial opportunities are limited, but anytime we make money, we like to see our filmmakers make money. A non-exclusive agreement can be very attractive to a filmmaker simply because it doesn't close any other opportunities. If another television, broadcast, or home video distributor would approach them they'd be completely free to take advantage of it. But on the flipside, if you do have someone that's representing you exclusively, there's an inherent driving factor for that company to get the maximum amount of exposure for your film. Additionally, we really benefit when our filmmakers get acclaim, success, and different types of distribution because it allows our viewers to get to know these film and say, Oh, I've heard of them and Amaze Films has it on this series or channel. We seek to benefit ourselves but want our filmmakers to excel because it really helps everyone.

"Filmmakers need to keep their options open. A lot of filmmakers jump on the first deal that comes their way because they don't think anything else will happen, but the reality is that there's not a window of opportunity that opens, then closes. If a film distributor has an interest in your film, their interest will continue. So keep your options open and do your homework. Filmmakers tend to be more production than promotion oriented. Filmmakers really have to be their own salespeople and do their research and learn about all the distribution outlets to figure out which one is best for their film."

Chip Taylor's exclusive agreements are usually three to five years in length, but include a "release" option.

"To assure producers that they won't get 'stuck' I offer producers a ninety-day release guarantee, should I ever not meet any terms of my agreement," says Chip. "In twenty years I have never had a producer use that ninety-day release, but it's good insurance for them. I have heard some producers' sad stories of having their title with a distributor who did nothing for them, and they couldn't get out of the agreement. Typically royalties are 20 to 25 percent for non-broadcast sales and 35 to 65 percent on broadcast, which is relatively standard. Many producers expect an advance on royalties. I have known too many producers who received their advance and then never received anything else after that. Be sure the agreement says the royalty is based on 'dollars received'; otherwise, there may be costs included by the distributors which allows them never to pay the producer any more money. I always pay producers based on gross dollars received."

## Finding the Right Distributor

As Ruben stated, filmmakers often agree to the first distribution deal that comes along for fear that nothing better will emerge. I once made that mistake (under a binding contract) with a short film, which went nowhere fast. A little wiser and sharper, I discovered Chip Taylor while shopping a documentary series. With nineteen years of experience under his belt, he is savvy but also—*shock*—honest and committed to his craft. He welcomes filmmakers to contact him if their projects are appropriate for his catalog.

"If I am not the right distributor for them, I will direct them to ones that I know," offers Chip. "Having been in the business so many years now, I know them all. I do this on a constant basis, so I feel it is a proper word of advice. In general, though, the Internet is a good place to start. A producer can see the Web sites of all the active distributors in the business.

"Once a producer is speaking with a distributor, it's vital that the producer see the agreement and go over it item by item. If you have any questions, don't hesitate to ask and get the answers you need. If you are not happy with the answers, trust your instinct and don't go with that distributor. Don't be so anxious to have a distribution deal that you sacrifice your best judgment. Today, with the Internet, there is no reason why a producer cannot be aligned with a distributor that is best suited for their project."

## Promotion through Distribution

The last thing you want to do is sign away rights on a project that never sees the light of day. When selecting a distributor, it is important to find out how they market and promote similar offerings.

"Our trailers are in a bunch of different places," says Ruben of Amaze Films' promotional strategy. "We advertise both a short series and feature series. In addition to working with Akimbo we also do a lot of print advertisement. If you look in *Filmmaker Magazine, MovieMaker*, or *Film Thread* you might see banners advertising our films. We also have screenings in Los Angeles and New York. We have an ongoing Los Angeles event called Scene, which takes place on Wednesdays at Cinespace where we showcase films from our catalog. It's a good opportunity for our filmmakers to get additional exposure. We have production companies, casting directors, and agents come out, so it's a very industry oriented event."

Chip's projects tend to fall in the non-broadcast realm, so he takes a different approach, investing a significant amount in sales, software, and promotional materials.

"I do work with certain PBS and independent stations to promote programs," he explains. "It is one way of getting sales. My twentieth anniversary catalogue went to thousands of educators, librarians, museums, medical institutions, and television programmers. We send out thousands of one-sheet press releases on an individual basis and enter certain programs into festivals. I have five salespeople who contact customers every business day of the year. I have invested over $200,000 in software, which allows us to provide custom-made proposals for each customer we contact. I believe in individualizing calls because each customer may have a different need, so our software assists with that. We allow all 'home use' customers to preview our programs at no charge, sending out thousands of previews a year. Lastly, of course, we invest daily in our Web site, *www.chiptaylor.com*, which includes full descriptions, awards, and review information."

## The Filmmaker/Distributor Relationship

A distributor, like your talent, crew, agent, manager, attorney, accountant, or PR rep, is invested in the success of your projects and should be considered an integral part of the team. Assuming a good experience, filmmakers typically return to the same distributor on future projects. Like any other relationship in the filmmaking process, relationships and trust are earned over time.

"*Trust* is the most important word between a producer and a distributor," Chip believes. "Good producers put their souls into a production when they create it. Being a producer myself, I know how much work it takes to complete a program. I encourage producers to send me their programs, short or long, and I will tell them the truth as to whether I think it has a chance to sell. Sadly, some very good programs may not sell a lot of copies. I also tell producers the truth about payment and reporting of royalties. I personally have invested over $150,000 over the years to be sure my royalty reporting software is 100 percent accurate and provides producers with the exact information they want to know about their programs and ensures they receive their royalties on time. My software shows who previewed, reviewed, purchased, or returned a program. This type of information cements a producer's trust. With me they know exactly how much marketing went into their program, and they see the sales results. I don't know any other distributor who provides this type of information, as it's not required, but I simply feel more comfortable sharing it so they can trust that they've given their 'baby' to someone who cares about it as much as they do.

"One reason my catalog has grown from twenty-six titles in 1985 to over 2000 is because so many producers remain with my company. I invest in my producers, not only marketing their programs and paying royalties, but also assisting them in ways to get other monies to produce more programs by connecting them with people I know who could help them complete their projects. It is almost impossible to produce just one program and make a living from that afterwards, so a producer needs to keep working. In return, producers who see this value-added benefit of working with me come back with more programs and often word of mouth brings other producers to my company."

## The Filmmaker's Responsibility

Having a distributor is rather like having an agent. While someone is in your corner to help market and distribute your film, it doesn't mean you can sit back and neglect it yourself.

"Producers know their programs better than anyone," Chip reminds us. "I encourage them to provide me with any information they may have so that my salespeople can follow up on their contacts. Also, I ask producers whenever they have the chance to use word of mouth to direct people to the Web site, then we can take it from there."

"They call filmmaking the War of Art for a reason," adds Ruben. "That phrase is poignant for me because art is about expression of one's self, but it's also about communication. I think a lot of filmmakers get pigeonholed into focusing on the expressive part. Filmmakers have to take it upon themselves to promote their films and make sure that they are getting festival exposure or television or home video exposure or word of mouth through film events in various cities, and they often attract a huge following because people want to see what the up-and-comers are up to. Sure it's about production and telling a good story but it's also about letting people know how to see your story, so it's a dichotomy that you must pursue."

## Short Film Opportunities

Filmmakers create thousands of shorts every year, knowing that there are few commercial opportunities. Prestigious international festivals and positive reviews can unfold some markets, especially outside of the United States, where screening venues may include TV, galleries, the Internet, planes, shops, clubs, cafes, bars, and mobile phones, although even these forms of exposure offer few financial benefits.

"It's very difficult with short films," Ruben acknowledges. "However, if filmmakers make a short film and spend years trying to recoup their money, they're really missing out on the opportunity of future projects. Short films are often a résumé piece, so filmmakers have to retain the balance between showing off their work and focusing on future projects. Historically speaking, when looking at the legends, they all started with small movies and micro budgets. Eventually it all paid off, so it's important for filmmakers to keep their future in mind."

"Short films help get the recognition that gives your intention to show you're doing the right thing and your processes are working and your approach is working," agrees Kerry Rock of Potoroo Films.

Despite the odds, there are significantly more opportunities for short films to get exposure compared to the recent past.

"Ten years ago there were miniscule, if not zero, outlets for short films," says Ruben. "Obviously the Internet has been the groundbreaker for the ability to screen video directly to consumers. It's shown that people really have an interest in seeing this programming.

"We definitely cater to the independent film audience so we have more opportunity for viewers to purchase from different types of avenues. Akimbo, for example, has a set-top box [like cable for your TV or PC] that consumers can buy to have access to thousands of hours of independent cinema. There are the traditional routes like home video, which we have some interest in with our Short Series. As far as television broadcast, a lot of the new programs that set up short films, such as A&E, Sundance Channel, HBO, Spike TV, and MTV are looking for films but have a shortage of good ones. So filmmakers who have good shorts can seek those broadcast routes and get some tremendous exposure. There's a short film that's part of our series called *Divali*, which is a South Asian identity film that was screened on PBS. They have a whole series of short films that's broken down by genre, one of which is identity. So this film was screened around forty times on PBS. That's an example of a student film that got a tremendous amount of exposure. Filmmakers definitely need to search which broadcasters or distributors are seeking their type of content.

"It's also important that filmmakers look toward the future. Continue to promote the project you have but know it's really a step toward something else you will make. Success breeds failure so you have to make films over and over again to learn every mistake that's possible, whether that's through your own wrongs or those of your friends, but until you figure out how to make things well, it's all a learning process."

## Foreign Distribution

Although thousands of movies are produced each year, only a small number of them account for most box office receipts. Indeed, most films do not make a full return on their investment from domestic box office revenues, so filmmakers rely on profits from other markets, such as broadcast and cable television, videocassette and DVD sales and rentals, and foreign distribution. In fact, major film companies are receiving a growing portion of their revenue from abroad.

Many countries, such as China, impose heavy taxes and restrictions (such as the amount of screen or airtime available for non-domestic screenings) on films from other countries. However, it is still worth exploiting foreign markets, as it only increases your audience and gives you a greater opportunity for financial return. Foreign distributors, like domestic, are listed in the Hollywood Distributors Directory.

# Summary

My hope is that the readers of this book gain as much from the experience of reading it as I did writing it. As I connected with talented filmmakers from around the globe, my respect for such brave and creative entrepreneurs grew and grew. It also helped me realize I wasn't alone in the pursuit of dreams and I have made some wonderful new friends as a result. While we are all distinctly different as film production company owners, we share much in common, from the frustration of administrative chores to the satisfaction of completing and distributing personally important projects.

Independent filmmakers often have difficulty finding equilibrium between the business and creative aspects of the craft. If you choose to start a film production company, those scales are even more tipped as you juggle accounting, legal, marketing, promotional, networking, and distribution tasks while simultaneously working like a madman to get your projects off the ground. Paying attention to all aspects, and seeking advice when necessary, will help your company grow and keep you focused on your goals.

A willingness to stay true to your vision is also critical. You will likely encounter difficult times and moments of doubt when you, and others, question your choices. You will also make countless mistakes in the process. As Emma Farrell of Six Foot High Films bluntly stated, "Be fully prepared for things to go hysterically and spectacularly wrong."

But mistakes can be invaluable learning opportunities that help prepare us for greater risks ahead. Ruba Nadda of Coldwater Productions understood this after making a series of short films before embarking on a full-length, saying, "I've made so many mistakes along the way. Now I'm prepared for a feature, as I won't make the same mistakes."

As I have shared, my personal experiences as a production company owner have ranged from truly fulfilling to downright grueling. But I wouldn't trade my career for any other job in the world. Although I don't know what the future holds, I'm living my dream in the "now." I hope you're living yours.

# About the Author

**Sara Caldwell, Amphion Productions, Santa Clarita, CA**

Since forming Amphion Productions in 1991, Sara has written and produced over two hundred film, television, documentary, Web site, and satellite teleconference projects for national and international clients, specializing in healthcare and education. She has also produced a number of her own documentaries on issues of disability, the importance of mentoring children, and the arts. Sara also teaches film production courses at the College of the Canyons in Valencia, California. She is a frequent workshop leader, guest speaker, and screenplay consultant.

As an award-winning screenwriter, Sara has written many articles on the screenwriting process and is co-author of *So You Want to Be a Screenwriter: How to Face the Fears and Take the Risks* (Allworth Press). She has optioned numerous screenplays and has developed feature and television scripts for production companies in Los Angeles and Chicago.

Sara has received many awards including first place in the Illinois/Chicago Screenwriting Competition and a Golden Apple in the International Educational Film/Video Festival.

Prior to forming Amphion Productions, Sara was a writer/producer for MotionMasters of Charleston, West Virginia, and at WORLDNET Television in Washington, D.C., where she wrote and produced live satellite video teleconferences for audiences in Africa, the Middle East, and East Asia.

Sara lives in Valencia, California, with her children, Dylan and Chloe.

# Participant Biographies

**Joni Brander, Brander Broadcast Communications, Chicago**

Joni Brander is a broadcast consultant based in Chicago and has worked in the broadcast industry since 1983. She coaches news talent, from the top ten to the smallest markets, as well as corporate executives, politicians, and students. Prior to founding BBC in 1992, Joni's experience included consulting for a major international consulting firm, stints with television stations, production crews, and host and talent for numerous productions. Joni served as the 1997–98 Visiting Professional at Ohio University's Scripps School of Journalism. She served as a panelist and presenter at several RTNDA national conventions. She also wrote the "Feedback" column for the RTNDA's Communicator from 1994 to 1997. *www.thetvcoach.com*

**Jamey Brumfield and David Birdwell, Your Plan B, Chicago**

Your Plan B was established in 1997 with the focus of helping clients build productive relationships with their audiences, using the Web and intranets as tools for exchange. Jamey and David believe that deepening relationships allows clients to accomplish a spectrum of age-old business goals, from brand awareness and collection of demographic information to building a system of interconnected revenue streams. Business goals vary, but they all begin with the audience. Their name, Your Plan B, happened by accident while Jamey was talking on the phone reminding a friend to have a Plan B in case his original plan flopped. David overheard her and his eyes lit up and said, "There—that is our name!" They always talk about and have a Plan B. *Plan 9 from Outer Space* happened to make a great theme for the site and as such they became *Your Plan B! A Smarter Brand of Web Development.* *www.yourplanb.com*

### Carole Dean, From the Heart Productions, Oxnard, CA

Thirty years ago Carole Dean took a $20 bill and turned it into a $50 million a year industry when she reinvented the tape and short-end industry in Hollywood. As the president and CEO of From the Heart Productions, Carole has produced over 100 television programs, including the popular cable program HealthStyles, where she interviewed some of the biggest names in the industry, including Dr. Deepak Chopra, Dr. Weil, and Dr. Caroline Myss. In 1992 Carole created the Roy W. Dean Grant Foundation in honor of her late father. Today Carole's grant and mentorship programs have provided millions of dollars in goods and services and have played an instrumental role in establishing the careers of some of the industry's most promising filmmakers. *www.fromtheheartproductions.com*

### Shuli Eshel, Eshel Productions, Chicago

Shuli Eshel, an Israeli-born Chicago filmmaker, is an award-winning producer/director of videos, films, and documentaries covering a myriad of subjects. From corporate and promotional pieces to socially significant documentaries, she brings a multitude of talent and vision to her art. She is former president of IFP/Midwest, a national organization of independent filmmakers. Shuli has been on the film and television faculties of Columbia College and Roosevelt University in Chicago as well as the Tel-Aviv Museum and College of Design in Israel. She holds a B.A. in English and American Literature and Linguistics from Tel-Aviv University and a Master of Fine Arts in Film and Television from Hornsey College of Art in London, England. She is president of Cavalcade Communications Group, a full-service video and film production company, and operates Eshel Productions. *www.cavalgroup.com*

## Emma Farrell, Six Foot High Films, Brighton, England

Emma Farrell started Six Foot High Films, Ltd. in 1998 after graduating from Manchester University with a Masters Degree in Anthropology and Film. Since its creation, the company has produced three low-budget features, five short films, and numerous commercials, including the multi-award-winning *Lost*. In 2001 they ran the international script writing competition "Six Foot Shorts" and now actively work with new writers to improve their craft, currently through their script and treatment consultancy service. They also work with other companies supplying directors, producers, and other expertise for commercials, corporate work, and shorts. In 2003 their short film *Cupboard Love* played at Film Festivals across the States and the UK, picking up the prestigious Gold Special Jury Award at WorldFest-Houston. They have just completed a stunning 35-mm cinemascope short film, *Homecoming*, and have a slate of five features in development. In the future they intend to build on their reputation for diverse high-quality products and increase the focus on developing and producing features. *www.sixfoothighfilms.com*

## Robert Hardy, Rainforest Films, Marietta, GA

In 1994 director Rob Hardy and producer William Packer created Rainforest Films on the eve of the success of their first film, *Chocolate City*. Rainforest Films grew into a full-service film and video production company that offers a wide range of quality services, concepts, and techniques, working within both the public and private sectors, entertainment and sporting events, music videos, corporate projects, and feature films. After *Chocolate City*, the partners produced their spellbinding film, *Trois*. Remarkably, the picture was funded, produced, and distributed entirely by African Americans. In its first weekend of theatrical release on twenty-two screens, *Trois* earned the highest per screen average of any film in the country. It went on to generate upwards of $1.3 million at the box office in just over ninety cities. Their company motto "Makin' Moves Y'all" is based on their strong belief in the necessity of continual motion. Anything not moving becomes stagnant. As the rainforest has endured for eons, Rainforest Films hopes to provide a comparable legacy. *www.rainforest-films.com*

## Michael Harpster, Marketing and Distribution Expert, Los Angeles

Michael Harpster is a thirty-year veteran of the film industry since starting his career with New Line Cinema in 1970. He was president of marketing at New Line for ten years and executive producer for three of the company's pictures. In 1999 he became president of marketing for Providence and is currently overseeing distribution for Constellation and Caliente Entertainment.

## Frey Hoffman, Freydesign Productions, Chicago

Freydesign Productions is a full-service production company based out of Chicago. They are committed to making motion pictures that have enduring aesthetic value and contribute meaningfully to the individuals, communities, organizations, and audiences for which they are created. Since their inception in 1997 the company has grown from working with local artists, entertainment, sports, business, nonprofit, and public interest organizations to national and international entities in the same fields. Their clients include Prevent Child Abuse America, American Hospital Association, BBC Americas, Ryerson-Tull, Center for Neighborhood Technology, BET Comics of the Month, DDB Tribal, and Sheila King Public Relations & Marketing. They have worked with NY Times Bestsellers, platinum selling recording artists, and many other individuals distinguished in their respective fields of work. Their work in production has been seen on The Discovery and Discovery Health Channels, Home & Garden Television, PBS, CBS, ABC, HBO and in video stores, homes, offices, and boardrooms nationwide and internationally. Currently, Freydesign is in the process of creating its own documentary-based content for distribution through national cable and television outlets. *www.freydesignproductions.com.*

## Lawrence P. Lundin, CPA, Chicago

Lawrence (Larry) Lundin, CPA, has been handling the accounting needs of Chicago area business and individuals for nearly twenty-five years. He joined Gerald M. Schechter & Company in 1979, becoming a partner in 1983 and remaining with the company until its dissolution in 1997. At that time he joined the ranks of small business owners and started his own firm, focusing on family owned businesses. Larry's clients range from construction and trade industries to retail and service ventures, with a special niche for creative entrepreneurs, such as media production and dance companies as well as theme restaurants. Larry is a graduate of DePaul University and lives in Chicago with his wife, Mary, and his son, Patrick.

### Ruba Nadda, Coldwater Films, Toronto, Canada

Ruba Nadda is a writer, director, and producer living in Toronto. She has written, produced, and directed twelve short films and two feature films. She is also a fiction writer, with many of her short stories published all over the world, in more than 400 journals such as *Riversedge Journal, West Wind Review 18th* Anthology, *The Sounds of Poetry, Blood & Aphorism, White Wall Review, Room of One's Own,* and *Wascana Review.* Ruba was selected as a Trailblazer in film by the ReelWorld Film Festival. Without any prior film experience, she was accepted into the Tisch School of the Arts, New York, where she completed her summer program and came back to Toronto to make films immediately. Her twelve short films have been shown in over 350 film festivals in five years. She has had over fifteen retrospectives of her work shown in numerous cities, including Rotterdam, Stockholm, Vienna, Wurzburg, Austin, San Francisco, Regina, Edmonton, Ottawa, Toronto, and Princeton University, where her films and technique are now part of their Film Theory curriculum. Ruba has been profiled in such publications as *Scarlett Magazine, Eye Magazine, Toronto Life Magazine, Toronto Star, Ooh La La on City TV, Take One Magazine, Toronto Sun,* the *West End Review,* the *Globe & Mail, Cosmopolitan, Elle Magazine,* the *Jerusalem Report,* and *Saturday Night Magazine (National Post). www.rubanadda.com*

### Bill Plympton, Plymptoons, New York City

Bill Plympton's short and feature films have been seen widely around the country, highlighting many animation festivals. His oblique, off-center sense of the ridiculous in everyday life has made the *Microtoons* and his other shorts a popular MTV offering. After Bill moved to New York City, a recent college graduate with a B.A. in graphic design, his illustrations began gracing the pages of the *New York Times, Vogue, House Beautiful,* the *Village Voice, Screw,* and *Vanity Fair.* His cartoons also appeared in *Viva, Penthouse, Rolling Stone, National Lampoon,* and *Glamour.* All his life Bill

Plympton has been fascinated by animation, but it wasn't until 1983 that he was approached to animate a film, *Boomtown*. Immediately following the completion of *Boomtown*, he began his own animated films, including *Your Face*, which garnered a 1988 Oscar nomination for Best Animation. After a string of highly successful short films, he began his first feature film. What came to be called *The Tune* was financed entirely by the animator himself. Next, Bill moved to live action. *J. Lyle*, his first live-action feature, is a wacky, surreal comedy about a sleazy lawyer who meets a magical talking dog that changes his life. After a successful festival circuit, *J. Lyle* was released in theaters around the country. Bill's second live-action feature, *Guns on the Clackamas*, is a behind-the-scenes look at an imaginary disastrous Western. In 1998, Bill completed another animated feature titled *I Married a Strange Person*, a heartwarming story of a newlywed couple on their wedding night. Bill's next animated feature, *Mutant Aliens*, the story of a stranded astronaut returning to Earth after twenty years in space, was completed in January 2001 and premiered at the Sundance Film Festival. Bill's latest film, *Hair High*, is a gothic '50s high school comedy about a love triangle that goes terribly bad, with two young murdered teens returning to their prom to get revenge. He charted new territory in animation by broadcasting all of his drawing for the film live on the web. *www.plymptoons.com*

### Diana Sole, MotionMasters, Charleston, WV

Diana is a veteran of the communications industry. A Marshall University Graduate, she has been president of MotionMasters since 1988 and prior to that served as its vice president and executive producer. With more than twenty years in the industry, she has produced hundreds of videos and commercials used to educate, motivate, and persuade. Prior to joining MotionMasters in 1984, Diana worked as a public relations account executive at Charles Ryan Associates, as promotional/public services director at WVAH-TV, and as a news producer at WOWK-TV. She served as the communications director and spokesperson for the 1996 campaign of former West Virginia Governor Cecil H. Underwood. In addition to numerous awards received by MotionMasters, Diana was a 1997 recipient of the State Journal's "Who's Who in West Virginia Business" award and was the winner of a 2001 Ernst & Young Entrepreneur of the Year Award. *www.motionmasters.com*

## Les Szekely, Secret's Out Productions, Cleveland, OH

Les Szekely is a film and video producer/director/writer/editor, as well as an actor and music composer. He has worked in both Hollywood and Cleveland, and is the founder of Secret's Out Productions, an independent production company. Les was a segment producer/director/writer for such shows as *America's Funniest Home Videos, America's Funniest People* (*ABC*), and *On the Television* (*Nickelodeon Network*). He won a National ACE Award and an Emmy Award for writing/directing/co-producing, *Yes, This Is Comedy*, a Mad TV-type sketch comedy show. As a filmmaker, Les wrote and directed *Vampire Time Travelers, I Know What You Did in English Class, Night of the Living Date*, and *The Not-So-Grim Reaper*. In addition, he co-produced *Amazon Warrior* and *Merchants of Death*, and starred in *Bloodstream, Vampire Night,* and *Monsters.com*. Most of these films are in worldwide distribution. Currently, Les hosts a radio talk show called B+ Moviemaking, which focuses on the art of making low-in-budget-yet-high-in-quality movies. He also teaches college courses in screenwriting and other media subjects.

## Kerry Rock and Georgina Willis, Potoroo Films, Sydney, Australia

Georgina Willis is a young writer/director who built an international reputation in photography before moving into film. Georgina has an Arts degree and a Masters degree from the University of Sydney. Writer/producer Kerry Rock has produced a range of films, including most recently her first feature film, *Watermark*. With degrees in arts and commerce, Kerry also has extensive experience in writing, film editing, and marketing. *www.potoroofilms.com*

## Brad Sykes, Nightfall Pictures, Los Angeles

Brad Sykes made eight feature-length projects on video before attending Boston University's film program in 1993. By the time he graduated cum laude in 1997, he had already worked for both Paramount Pictures and Ridley Scott's Scott Free Productions. After moving to Los Angeles, Sykes continued to work in film in various capacities both here and abroad (a brief stint at Castel Film, Romania) before landing his first writing-directing job in 1998. By 2000, he was writing and directing full-time, with many genre credits such as *Camp Blood 1 + 2, Mad Jack*, and *The Coven* under his belt. Brad has continued to make his mark with more recent projects like *Death Factory* and *Demon's Kiss*. Many of his films have been distributed worldwide at Cannes, AFM, and MIFED and can be found at rental outlets such as Blockbuster and Hollywood Video. Brad's films have also been reviewed in, among others, *Fangoria, Rue Morgue, Videoscope, LA Weekly*, and the French *Mad Movies*. Brad is known for pushing the horror genre into new and challenging directions while still delivering maximum thrills and chills. His latest film, *Goth*, is a psychological thriller that delves into the underbelly of the Goth subculture. Brad lives in Los Angeles with his wife, screenwriter Josephina Sykes.

## Chip Taylor, Chip Taylor Communications, Derry, NH

In the early 1970s Chip Taylor was an elementary school teacher. He then spent ten years working for Journal Films, a pioneering educational film distributor of the day. After the company owner died, Chip began his own distribution company, Apropos Studios, officially changed to Chip Taylor Communications in 1985. Chip takes great pride in his company's slate of offerings and often says "our company doesn't just sell DVD or video, we sell content." *www.chiptaylor.com*

## Jerry Vasilatos, Nitestar Productions, Los Angeles

Jerry Vasilatos formed Nitestar Productions in Chicago and moved the company to Los Angeles in 1996. His company projects include the comedy spoof *The Blair Witch Rejects*, which he directed, and the award-winning documentary *A Refugee and Me*, co-produced with director Kevin Leadingham. Prior to his move from Chicago, Jerry wrote, produced, and directed the independent holiday drama *Solstice,* which was broadcast nationally as Lifetime Television's Original World Premiere Movie during Christmas of 1994. *Solstice* was awarded the Silver Award by the Charleston International Film Festival, the Bronze Award by the Houston International Film Festival, and was broadcast again by Lifetime Television on Christmas Eve of 1995. It was released on home video in October of 1997 by Monument Entertainment. Jerry is a graduate of Columbia College in Chicago, where he earned his Bachelor's Degree in film and also served as the president of their West Coast Alumni chapter. *www.nitestar.com*

# Organizations and Suggested Reading

## Organizations

**The American Film Institute (AFI).** A national organization dedicated to advancing and preserving film, television, and other forms of the moving image. Their programs promote innovation and excellence through teaching, presenting, preserving, and redefining the art form. *www.afi.com*

**American Film Marketing Association (AFMA).** A trade association for the independent motion picture and television industry. They provide marketing support services such as the American Film Market (AFM). *www.afma.com*

**Association of Independent Feature Film Producers (AIFFP).** A nonprofit educational and advocacy organization based in Hollywood dedicated to the advancement of the business of independent feature film production. *www.aiffp.org/index.html*

**Association of Independent Video & Filmmakers.** A membership organization serving international film and video makers, from documentarians and experimental artists to makers of narrative features. *www.aivf.org*

**The Empowerment Project.** Provides facilities, training, and other support for independent producers, artists, activists, and organizations working in video and other electronic media. Its purpose is to work toward democratizing access to the media, and to provide the resources necessary to put the power of media in the hands of individuals and organizations working to further important social and artistic purposes. *www.empowermentproject.org*

**Film Arts Foundation.** One of the nation's top resource centers for independent filmmakers, offering a film festival, an exhibition, education, grants and fiscal sponsorship programs, and an equipment rental facility. Also publishes *Release Print* magazine. *www.filmarts.org*

**The Film-Makers' Cooperative.** The largest archive and distributor of independent and avant-garde films in the world. Created by artists in 1962, the Coop has more than 5000 films and videotapes in its collection. *www.film-makerscoop.com*

**Independent Documentary Association (IDA).** A non-profit member organization providing publications, benefits, and a public forum on issues of nonfiction film, video, and multimedia.

**Independent Feature Project (IFP).** A non-profit member organization dedicated to providing resources, information, and avenues of communication for independent filmmakers, industry professionals, and independent film enthusiasts. IFP's six chapters are located in Chicago, Los Angeles, Miami, Minneapolis/St. Paul, New York, and Seattle, but serves members nationwide. *www.ifp.org*

**Independent Television Service (ITVS).** Funds, distributes, and promotes new programs produced by independent producers primarily for public television. They like proposals that take creative risks, explore complex issues, and express points of view seldom seen on commercial or public television

**Latino Public Broadcasting.** Funds projects through a competitive grant proposal process. Decisions about which projects are funded are made by an independent panel of broadcast professionals. *www.lpbp.org*

**National Asian American Telecommunications Association (NAATA).** Offers a media fund, made possible with funds from Corporate Public Broadcasting (CPB), to increase visibility of Asian-American programs on public television and the way in which Asian Americans are perceived and understood. *www.naatanet.org/community/index.html*

**National Black Programming Consortium.** Funds, commissions, acquires, and awards talented makers of quality African-American film and video projects. Selected programs reflect a variety of subjects and production styles. NBPC funds every phase of the production process. *www.nbpc.tv/index.php*

**National Endowment for the Humanities (NEH).** An independent grant-making agency of the U.S. government dedicated to supporting research, education, and public programs in the humanities. Projects must address significant figures, events, or developments in the humanities and draw their content from humanities scholarship. *www.neh.gov*

**Native American Public Telecommunication, Inc. (NAPT).** Proposals are requested for programs in many genres including documentary, performance, cultural/public affairs, children's, and animation. The NAPT Public Television Program Fund is made possible by funding provided by the CPB. *www.nativetelecom.org/index.html*

**Sundance Institute.** Founded by Robert Redford and dedicated to the development of emerging screenwriters and directors of vision, and to the national and international exhibition of new, independent dramatic and documentary films. *http://institute.sundance.org*

## Magazines (Print and Online)

**American Cinematographer.** Offers in-depth, behind-the-scenes articles and interviews with cinematographers and directors. *www.theasc.com/magazine*

**Boxoffice Magazine.** Includes reviews, interviews, and articles covering the film industry. *www.boxoff.com*

**Bright Lights.** A quarterly film journal on movie analysis, history, and commentary, looking at classic and commercial, independent, exploitation, and international film from a wide range of vantage points from the aesthetic to the political. *www.brightlightsfilm.com*

**Cineaste.** Quarterly magazine published since 1967 that features contributions from many of America's most articulate and outspoken writers, critics, and scholars on the art and politics of cinema. *www.cineaste.com*

**Film Comment.** Published bi-monthly by the Film Society of Lincoln Center, this magazine offers reviews and commentary on international films, American movies, the avant-garde, and more. *www.filmlinc.com/fcm/fcm.htm*

**Film Journal.** Includes reviews, news, and interviews for Hollywood, independent, and foreign films. *www.filmjournal.com*

**Film Threat.** Champions the increasingly popular explosion of independent and underground films via their Web site and free weekly e-mail. *www.filmthreat.com*

**Filmmaker Magazine.** Gives an insider's perspective on the world of independent filmmaking. *www.filmmakermagazine.com*

**Hollywood Reporter.** Considered the industry's most complete daily entertainment news and information source for over seventy years. *www.hollywoodreporter.com*

**iF Magazine.** Focused on news, reviews, and information on independent filmmaking. *www.ifmagazine.com*

**Inside Film Magazine.** A comprehensive directory of the world's film festivals. *www.insidefilm.com*

**Millimeter.** A professional resource for production and post. *www.millimeter.com*

**Movieline Magazine.** Reviews, features, interviews, and awards coverage. *www.movieline.com*

**MovieMaker Magazine.** A guide to the art and business filmmaking. *www.moviemaker.com*

**Premiere Magazine.** Includes interviews, reviews, independent film coverage, and news. *www.premiere.com*

**Preview.** International quarterly publication on upcoming studio and independent movie releases. *www.preview-online.com*

**Screen International.** Weekly news for film business professionals, carrying in-depth features on the global film business, weekly production listings from foreign territories, and worldwide box office statistics. *www.screendaily.com*

**Sight and Sound.** The British Film Institute's monthly publication providing news from around the globe, with special correspondents reporting on film, television, the Internet, gaming, and new technology. *www.bfi.org.uk/sightandsound*

**Urban Cinefile.** An online magazine devoted to Australian cinema. *www.urbancinefile.com*

**Variety.** A premier source of entertainment news since 1905. *www.variety.com*

## Books

Adelman, Kim. *The Ultimate Filmmaker's Guide to the Short Film: Making it Big in Shorts.* Studio City, Calif.: Michael Wiese Productions, 2004.

Avrich, Barry. *Selling the Sizzle*: *The Magic and Logic of Entertainment Marketing.* Los Angeles: Maxworks Publishing Group, 2002.

Barbash, Ilisa and Lucien Taylor. *Cross-Cultural Filmmaking: A Handbook for Making Documentary and Ethnographic Films and Videos.* Berkeley and Los Angeles: University of California Press, 1997.

Cones, John. *The Feature Film Distribution Deal: A Critical Analysis of the Single Most Important Film Industry Agreement.* Carbondale: Southern Illinois University Press, 1996.

Cones, John. *Film Finance & Distribution: A Dictionary of Terms.* Los Angeles: Silman-James Press, 1992.

Cones, John. *43 Ways to Finance Your Feature Film: A Comprehensive Analysis of Film Finance.* Carbondale: Southern Illinois University Press, 1998.

Dean, Carole. *The Art of Funding Your Film: Alternative Financing Concepts.* Los Angeles: Dean Publishing, 2003.

Donaldson, Michael. *Clearance and Copyright: Everything the Independent Filmmaker Needs to Know.* Los Angeles: Silman-James Press, 2003.

Durie, John, Annika Pham, and Neil Watson. *Marketing & Selling Your Film around the World: A Guide for Independent Filmmakers.* Los Angeles: Silman-James Press, 2000.

Edwards, Paul and Sarah Edwards. *Working from Home: Everything You Need to Know about Living and Working under the Same Roof.* New York: Jeremy P. Tarcher/Putnam, 1999.

Gaspard, John and Dale Newton. *Persistence of Vision: An Impractical Guide to Producing a Feature Film for under $30,000.* Studio City, Calif.: Michael Wiese Productions, 1999.

Hampe, Barry. *Making Documentary Films and Reality Videos: A Practical Guide to Planning, Filming, and Editing Documentaries of Real Events.* New York: Owl Books, 1997.

Harmon, Renee and James Lawrence. *The Beginning Filmmaker's Guide to a Successful First Film.* New York: Walker & Company, 1997.

Koster, Robert. *The Budget Book for Film and Television.* Oxford: Focal Press, 2004.

Lee, John. *The Producer's Business Handbook.* Oxford: Focal Press, 2000.

Levison, Louise. *Filmmakers and Financing: Business Plans for Independents.* Oxford: Focal Press, 2003.

Litwak, Mark. *Contracts for the Film and Television Industry.* Los Angeles: Silman-James Press, 1994.

Schreibman, Myrl. *Indie Producers Handbook: Creative Producing From A to Z.* Hollywood: ifilm Publishing, 2001.

Simens, Dov. *From Reel to Deal: Everything You Need to Create a Successful Independent Film.* New York: Warner Books, 2003.

# Index

# Books from Allworth Press

Allworth Press is an imprint of Allworth Communications, Inc. Selected titles are listed below.

**Producing for Hollywood, Second Edition**
*by Paul Mason and Don Gold* (paperback, 6 × 9, 288 pages, $19.95)

**Shoot Me: Independent Filmmaking from Creative Concept to Rousing Release**
*by Roy Frumkes and Rocco Simonelli* (paperback, 6 × 9, 240 pages, 56 b&w illus., $19.95)

**Hollywood Dealmaking: Negotiating Talent Agreements**
*by Dina Appleton and Daniel Yankelevits* (paperback, 6 × 9, 256 pages, $19.95)

**Documentary Filmmakers Speak**
*by Liz Stubbs* (paperback, 6 × 9, 240 pages, $19.95)

**Making Your Film for Less Outside the U.S.**
*by Mark DeWayne* (paperback, 6 × 9, 272 pages, $19.95)

**Technical Film and TV for Nontechnical People**
*by Drew Campbell* (paperback, 6 × 9, 256 pages, $19.95)

**The Filmmaker's Guide to Production Design**
*by Vincent LoBrutto* (paperback, 6 × 9, 216 pages, 15 b&w illus., $19.95)

**Making Independent Films: Advice from the Filmmakers**
*by Liz Stubbs and Richard Rodriguez* (paperback, 6 × 9, 224 pages, 42 b&w illus., $16.95)

**The Health & Safety Guide for Film, TV & Theater**
*by Monona Rossol* (paperback, 6 × 9, 256 pages, $19.95)

**Directing for Film and Television, Revised Edition**
*by Christopher Lukas* (paperback, 6 × 9, 256 pages, 53 b&w illus., $19.95)

**Surviving Hollywood: Your Ticket to Success**
*by Jerry Rannow* (paperback, 6 × 9, 224 pages, $16.95)

**Creative Careers in Hollywood**
*by Laurie Scheer* (paperback, 6 × 9, 240 pages, $19.95)